# LOTUS 1-2-3
## Training Guide
## Version 2.2

**Graham Taylor**

Pitman

PITMAN PUBLISHING
128 Long Acre, London, WC2E 9AN
A Division of Longman Group UK Limited

© Graham Taylor 1991

First published in Great Britain 1991

**British Library Cataloguing in Publication Data**

Taylor, Graham
  Training guide – Lotus 1–2–3
  1. Microcomputer systems. Spreadsheet packages:
  Lotus 123
  1. Title.
  005.369

ISBN 0 273 03037 X

Typeset by ↗\ Tek Art Ltd, Addiscombe, Croydon, Surrey
Printed and bound in Great Britain

# Contents

# Acknowledgement

With thanks to Bill Smith for the use of his exercise in Task 26.

# Introduction

## What is a spreadsheet package?

A spreadsheet is the electronic equivalent of an accountant's ledger - a large piece of paper divided by vertical columns and horizontal rows into a grid of *cells*. The name derives from *spreading* the organisation's accounts on a sheet of paper so that the user can directly enter numbers, formulae or text into the cells.

Each cell is referred to by its coordinates, like a map-reference or point on a graph e.g. cell C12 is in column C row 12. Formulae can be entered to link cells (e.g. B1*C1 multiplies the contents of cells B1 and C1) so that the spreadsheet becomes a screen-based calculator. N.B. Some spreadsheet packages reference cells as, for example, r3c12, i.e. row 3, column 12.

**What if analysis**

Any figure can be changed at any time and the new results will be automatically shown. This is called 'what if' analysis e.g. *what if* sales go up by 10%? It is this facility to quickly recalculate figures which makes spreadsheets such powerful, useful and popular programs. Data can be converted into graphs of various types and printed out.

**Some uses of spreadsheets**

Spreadsheets are flexible modelling tools which can be adapted for many jobs involving repetitive numerical calculations, for example:
- Financial plans and budgets can be represented as a table, with columns for time periods (e.g. months) and rows for different elements of the plan (e.g. costs and revenues).
- Tax, investment and loan calculations.
- Statistics e.g. average, standard deviation, time series and regression analysis (in-built functions are included).
- Consolidation - merging branch or departmental accounts to form group (consolidated) accounts. This involves merging two or more worksheets together.
- Currency conversion - useful for an organisation with overseas interests such as a multi-national company.

## LOTUS 1-2-3 version 2.2

LOTUS 1-2-3 is an integrated business applications package combining a spreadsheet with graphics and data management. Most of what you do in 1-2-3 depends on the spreadsheet so these basic skills must be learnt first. We will look at graphics and databases later.

LOTUS 1-2-3 is the best-selling microcomputer package to date.

**System requirements**

Version 2.2 requires:
- an IBM or IBM-compatible personal computer
- 2 diskette drives *or* a hard disk and diskette drive
- a monochrome or colour monitor
- a keyboard
- 320k of main memory (more can be supported)
- version 2.0 of the Disk Operating System (DOS) or higher

LOTUS 1-2-3 version 2.2 is sold with a package called ALLWAYS which enables you to format and print your work in a variety of ways. LOTUS refers to it as the spreadsheet publishing add-in!

You cannot use ALLWAYS on a 2-diskette system and a minimum of 512k of main memory is needed.

This guide assumes that LOTUS 1-2-3 has been installed on the hard disk in a subdirectory called C:123 and that there is an executable file called 123 in this subdirectory. This means that LOTUS can be loaded automatically from the operating system prompt.

**Conventions used throughout the guide.**

Function keys are given their 1-2-3 name and shown in black boxes. e.g. Help `F1`

Key names including the sign `+` mean that you must press and hold down the first key and the second key together. e.g. `CTRL + ←` (i.e. Control key with left arrow key).

Key names separated by a space mean press one key and then press the second. e.g. `END` `HOME`

Information that you are to type in appears in bold typeface.

e.g. **INTEREST RATE CALCULATION**

The Enter key is used throughout the book; the Return key does the same job. Press the Enter key whenever you see the symbol `ENTER`

# Task 1

## Starting 1-2-3 and looking around the spreadsheet screen

**Objectives**

To get you started in 1-2-3
To become familiar with the worksheet screen
To move around the worksheet
To use 1-2-3 menus
To change the file directory
To look at the Help system

**Instructions**

Getting started in 1-2-3
From the DOS C> prompt:
Type **CD \ 123** ENTER to enter the 123 subdirectory.
Type **123** ENTER to get into LOTUS 1-2-3.
After some time the access menu will appear and 1-2-3 will be highlighted. Press the
ENTER key and a blank spreadsheet will appear. Note how different parts of the
screen show useful information. Keep your eyes on it when you work with 1-2-3.

Control panel

Cell address    Format    Column width    Cell contents    Column letter                    Mode indicator

                                                                                                        MENU
B11: (,0) [W10] +B8-B9
Worksheet  Range   Copy   Move   File   Print  Graph   Data   System  Add-In  Quit
Global     Insert  Delete Column Erase  Titles Window  Status Page    Learn
           A            B          C         D         E        F        G
1                             SUE,GRABBIT and RUN
2
3                        Q1        Q2        Q3        Q4       YEAR
4
5    Sales income     100000    120000    150000    170000    540000
6    Cost of sales     60000     70000     90000    100000    320000
7                   --------------------------------------------------
8    Gross Profit      40000     50000     60000     70000    220000
9    Overheads         15000     18000     22500     25500     81000
10                  --------------------------------------------------
11   Net Profit       |25,000|   32,000    37,500    44,500   139,000
12                  ==================================================
13
14                         Cell pointer and current cell
15
16
17
18
19
20
31-Jul-90  11:10 AM                                                    SCROLL

Row number          Date and time indicator                  Status indicator

The display screen
The 1-2-3 display screen is made up of:
*   **the worksheet** – a grid of columns and rows.
    This is where 1-2-3 stores and organises data.

1

- **a control panel** – 3 lines showing the menu choices and other information about your work and what 1-2-3 is doing.
  This is used for communication and interactive purposes.
  Line 1 gives the cell address, contents, format and protection status and column width.
  To the right is the **mode indicator** (READY, MENU, WAIT etc) which changes to tell you what state 1-2-3 is in.
  Line 2 is where you will see your typing. If 1-2-3 prompts for input you will see it here. Menu selections are displayed on line 2 also.
  Line 3 is 1-2-3's comment line for messages (e.g. sub-menus, instructions)
- **a status line** – the last line on screen showing date and time, any error messages and status indicators, e.g. UNDO tells you that you can cancel changes; CAPS denotes that the CAPS LOCK key is on.

## The worksheet

The entire worksheet is too large to fit on your screen. There are 256 columns (lettered A..Z, AA..AZ, BA..BZ up to IV) and 8192 rows (numbered 1..8192). However, you will soon see how easy it is to move to any part of the spreadsheet that you need.

The intersection of every column and row is called a cell. Each cell is referenced by a column letter(s) followed by a row number. This is its cell address e.g. A1,B7,DR99.

The rectangular bar which highlights the position of the **current cell** is called the **cell pointer.**

---

**Activity 1.1**

Moving around the worksheet
The pointer can be moved from cell to cell with the pointer-movement (arrow) keys which are on the right-hand side of your keyboard.
To use these keys ensure that NUM LOCK is off. Many keyboards have a light above the key showing whether it is on or off. Press it if it is on.
Press each of the arrow keys ← → ↓ ↑ in turn for practise.
Press F5 (the goto function key) and type **AA99** ENTER
The cell pointer is now in cell AA99. You can jump directly to any cell in the spreadsheet this way.
Press the HOME key. This will return you to the top left cell (A1).
Press END → (End then right arrow). This will move you to IV1 – the top right of your spreadsheet.
Press END ↓ (End then down arrow). This will take you to the bottom right corner i.e. cell IV8192.
Note that when your spreadsheet contains entries the END → and END ← keys will take you to the borders of your spreadsheet work - known as the **active area**. This is the point at which cell entries finish and blank cells appear. Conversely if you are in a blank area, these keys will stop at the first non-blank cell.
Press HOME to return to A1.
You can jump a screen (page) at a time by using these keys:

      PGUP – moves up      TAB – moves right
      PGDN – moves down      SHIFT+TAB – moves left

Moving the cell pointer off the end of the displayed worksheet either vertically or horizontally is known as scrolling. As you scroll, new columns or row labels will appear and others will go away. Do not panic: you can always get back to them. Out of sight does not mean they are lost!

**Activity 1.2**      Using 1-2-3 menus and selecting commands

Most tasks in 1-2-3 require you to select commands from menus which appear in the control panel when you press **/** (the slash key).

- Menus have a multi-level structure. While only one level at a time is shown, more than one selection may often be necessary.
- There are 2 methods of choosing a command.

   **Point** You can use the cursor keys →  ←  HOME  END to move and highlight the command that you want.

   Press ENTER to select the command highlighted.

   This method is recommended for beginners. It takes a little longer but you can see information about your chosen command on the line below. This will either be a sub-menu or a description of the command.

   **Type** You can type the first character of the command.

If you make a mistake or change your mind press the ESC (Escape) key to return to the previous menu.

Selection will cause changes in the control panel. A new menu will appear on line 2 and new comments on line 3. You can continue to make selections or use ESC to go back one step at a time.

CTRL + BREAK will cancel all of the **command sequence** at once.

More than one menu selection represents a command sequence.

Try the following simple example.

Changing the current directory

Request the main menu by pressing **/** (the slash key).

Highlight **F**(ile) and then **D**(irectory) by using the arrow keys and pressing ENTER.

Type: **C:\ 123** ENTER (or the drive letter and directory name that you want).

Press ESC if you are happy with the present directory or if you have made a mistake.

Files will now be saved to and retrieved from the 123 directory on drive C.


Getting Help in 1-2-3

Press the Help key F1

Highlight a topic, then press ENTER. Experiment as you wish.

Press ESC (the Escape key) to leave Help.

As you begin to master the package you will find the Help facility increasingly useful. It is a 'context-sensitive' Help i.e. it tries to help you wherever you need it.

From now on keystroke instructions will tell you to select a command as follows:

e.g. Press **/** (the slash key) **Q**(uit) **Y**(es) to leave 1-2-3. Use this whenever you wish to finish a session.

It is your choice whether to point and press ENTER or type the first character of the command. Remember the point method is best for beginners.

---

**Key words**
\
ESC
CTRL + BREAK
F1 (Help key)

## Task 2    **Basic data entry**

To learn to enter text (labels), numbers (values) and a formula by completing a simple activity.

**Instructions**

Type **123** and wait for the 1-2-3 system to be loaded into main memory.

The menu-line should display the access system command menu with 1-2-3 highlighted.

Press the **ENTER** key (Return on some keyboards) to select 1-2-3 — the spreadsheet option.

You will now be faced with an empty spreadsheet, with the cell in the top left-hand corner highlighted by the cell pointer. Any entry you make will be typed on the second line of the screen and entered into the cell which contains the cursor when you press **ENTER**

**Activity**

Entering labels, values and formulae

In A1 Type **DATA ENTRY DEMONSTRATION** and press **ENTER**

Note how the text extends beyond 9 characters of the cell.

Press **↓** **↓** ('down arrow' twice), type **SALES** and press **↓** ('down arrow'). Note how this last action entered the text *and* moved down.

Type **COST** and press **↓** 'down arrow'.

Type **PROFIT** and press **→** 'right arrow'. The cursor should now be in cell B5.

Type **+B3-B4** and press **↑** 'up arrow'. You have just entered a formula! 1-2-3 however just shows you its result, and as there are no values in B3 and B4, in this case it is zero.

Type a number into B4, press **↑** 'up arrow', then type another number into B3, and press **ENTER**

You now have a spreadsheet with **labels** (in A1, A3 and A4), **values** (in B3 & B4) and a **formula** to be evaluated (in B5). On a micro scale this is what spreadsheets are all about. Try altering the figures in the SALES and COST cells; use the arrow-keys to position the cell cursor, type a value and press **ENTER** or **↓** 'down arrow' to insert it. Note how PROFIT is immediately recalculated.

In general you can enter **one** of three items in a cell:

- a value
    - data which can be used in calculations
    - must start with a number $0..9 + - . \$$
    - scientific notation (e.g. $1.234E+06$)
    - may end with a percent sign (%)
- a formula
    - mathematical formulae or functions that compute values
    - must indicate a mathematical operation e.g. $(10+5)*A1$
    - must start as a number entry or with $@ \# + -$.
    - 1-2-3 has many built-in functions for statistical, financial and other work. They begin with the @ sign e.g. @ SUM(B4..F4) will add the contents of cells B4 through to F4.
- a label
    - titles or text in alphanumeric characters which makes the information understandable
    - can contain any string of characters or numbers
    - may start with any character except those which indicate a number or a formula or are otherwise used by 1-2-3 (e.g. **/**)
    - may be up to 240 characters long

— may display across several worksheet columns.
   If the next column is occupied, 1-2-3 will display as many
   characters as possible and store the rest.
— to ensure a label make the first symbol a Label-Prefix character.
   These position the label in the cell as follows:

| | |
|---|---|
| ' apostrophe | left-justify text (default) |
| " double quote | right-justify |
| ˆ caret | centre |

To demonstrate this type '**SALES**
                       "**COSTS**
                       ˆ**PROFITS** in A1, A3 and A4 respectively
and see how they are positioned in the cells. Remember the **ENTER** and/or ↓
(down arrow) key after each entry.

---

| Key words | Value |
|---|---|
| | Formula |
| | Label |

Task 3      **Working with files**

To save, retrieve and erase files from disk

---

**Activity 3.1**      Saving a file
Since the speadsheet in Task 2 is your first 1-2-3 spreadsheet, you are advised to save it.
Press **/** (the slash key), then look at the menu at the top of the screen. Press ⟶ 'right arrow' until **File** is highlighted and press ENTER
Press **S** (for Save) then type in a filename e.g. **DEMO1** (keep filenames short) and press ENTER
Filenames can be up to eight characters long with no spaces.
Note again how **/** puts you into the 1-2-3 COMMAND MENU display. The upper line offers you a selection of commands, the lower one, the set of options available within the highlighted command.
Select **/W**(orksheet) **E**(rase) **Y**(es) This will clear the screen for further work.

---

**Activity 3.2**      Retrieving a file
Your file is now on disk so you can bring it back at any time.
Select **/F**(ile) **R**(etrieve) and highlight the filename then press ENTER. Your spreadsheet will be called from disk on to the screen.
If there are a number of files it is better to press F3 (function key 3). This will show a full screen menu of filenames.
You can either type the filename that you require or highlight it using the pointer keys and pressing ENTER

---

**Activity 3.3**      Erasing a file
For good housekeeping delete this file from disk.
With DEMO1 in use, select **/F**(ile) **E**(rase) **W**(orksheet) **Y**(es).
Repeat Activity 3.1 to clear the screen.

---

**Key words**      F3 (File list)

## Task 4     **Editing and correcting mistakes**

**Objectives**    To make simple changes using the edit function key (`F2`)

**Instructions**    The edit function key (`F2`)

If a cell entry is incorrect or needs updating it is usually convenient just to retype it and overwrite the original. However, the edit function key provides a quick way of changing entries.

---

**Activity 4.1**

In cell A1 Type **This is a big mustake** `ENTER`
Press `F2`
Use the arrow key to move to u. Press `INS` (Insert key) to turn INSERT **off**. The OVR-overtype mode indicator will be displayed. Type **i** and press `ENTER`
When you press `F2` the cell entry contents will appear on line 2 of the control panel. The arrow (cursor) keys can be used to move around the entry. The `DEL` key deletes the character at the cursor, while the `BACK SPACE` key deletes the character at the left of the cursor. The `INS` key switches between inserting text, by moving existing text to the right, and replacing existing text. Press the `ENTER` key when complete.
Practise typing long labels into cells and editing them.

---

**Activity 4.2**

Using UNDO
Press `ALT+F4` (the UNDO feature).
Press `ALT+F4` again.
The UNDO will cancel the most recent change made in your worksheet. Pressing it again will restore your last change.

---

**Key words**

`F2` (Edit)
`ALT + F4` (Undo)

# Task 5    **Copying and moving**

**Objectives**

To copy cells using the copy command
To move cells' contents to different cells

**Instructions**

When formulae are copied or moved the cell addresses are automatically adjusted to the new cell location.

---

**Activity 5.1**

Copying
**▮C**opy creates copies of existing cell entries
1 Position the cell pointer in the cell(s) to be copied.
2 Select **▮**C(opy).
   1-2-3 will prompt: Enter range to copy FROM:
   Highlight the range of cells to copy and press **ENTER** to accept the range at the command line prompt.
3 1-2-3 will prompt: Enter range to copy TO:
   Move the cell pointer to the beginning of the target range and press **.** (full stop) to anchor the cell pointer. Then move it to the last cell in the TO range. The range of cells that you wish to copy TO: should now be highlighted. Press **ENTER** to confirm this.

---

**Instructions**

Absolute, relative and mixed copying
Before copying formulae, be sure you understand these terms.

**Relative addressing**
This records the position of each cell relative to the cell containing the formula. For example:
Type any eight numbers into cells B5 to E6.
In B7 type **+B5+B6** (this simply adds the contents of B5 and B6).
**▮C**(opy) FROM B7 TO **C7. .E7** Move to C7 and anchor the range with . (full stop).
Then **→** (right arrow) to highlight cells C7, D7, E7 **ENTER**. Move the cell pointer along row 7 and note the change in formula; e.g. in E7 it becomes +E5+E6 - the relative position has been kept.

**Absolute addressing**
If, however, the reference to a specific cell needs to be kept then an absolute address is necessary. In 1-2-3 this is done by using the **$** sign which ensures that the cell address does not change. Hence $B$7 indicates a permanent link to the value of column B row 7 wherever you copy it to.

**Mixed addressing**
It is quite possible to have a mixture of relative and absolute addressing. Hence $B7 indicates that the column reference should remain the same but the rows should change; B$7 will have the reverse effect.

**Activity 5.2**    Mixed copying

The following example demonstrates mixed copying (check your work with the results below):

In A1 type **INTEREST RATE CALCULATION**

In B2 type **0.1**

In C2 type **0.12**

In D2 type **0.14**

Select **/R**(ange) **F**(ormat) **P**(ercent) **0** and press **ENTER**

Press ⬅ ⬅ (left arrow key twice) to highlight the range B2..D2 then press **ENTER**

You now have these figures in percentage form.

In A4 type **10000** ⬇

In A5 type **30000** ⬇

In A6 type **50000** **ENTER**

Move to B4 and type **$A4*B$2** **ENTER**

1000 should appear (i.e. 10% of £10000)

Now copy this formula into the other cells.

With the pointer in B4 select **/C**(opy)

1-2-3 will prompt: Enter range to copy FROM:B4. .B4

Press **ENTER** to accept this.

1-2-3 will then prompt: Enter range to copy TO:

Press . (full stop) to anchor the pointer.

Press ➡ ➡ (arrow right twice) to go to D4.

Press ⬇ ⬇ (arrow down twice) to go to D6.

The range B4...D6 will now be highlighted.

Press **ENTER** to accept this.

All the calculations will appear on your spreadsheet. Check the formulae in the cells and see how 1-2-3 has adjusted them.

Your spreadsheet should look like the following.

```
INTEREST RATE CALCULATION
                    10%        12%        14%

        10000      1000       1200       1400
        30000      3000       3600       4200
        50000      5000       6000       7000


A1:  'INTEREST RATE CALCULATION
B2:  (P0) 0.1
C2:  (P0) 0.12
D2:  (P0) 0.14
A4:  10000
B4:  +$A4*B$2
C4:  +$A4*C$2
D4:  +$A4*D$2
A5:  30000
B5:  +$A5*B$2
C5:  +$A5*C$2
D5:  +$A5*D$2
A6:  50000
B6:  +$A6*B$2
C6:  +$A6*C$2
D6:  +$A6*D$2
```

**Activity 5.3**

Moving

**/M**(ove) will move a range of cells from one part of the worksheet to another.

It works in the same way as the COPY command with 1-2-3 prompting for FROM and TO ranges.

Try moving the work you have just created.

Press the `HOME` key to move to A1.

Select **/M**(ove).

1-2-3 will prompt: Enter range to move FROM:

Press `→` `→` `→` to D1.

Press `↓` `↓` `↓` `↓` `↓` to D6.

The range A1..D6 should now be highlighted.

Press `ENTER` to accept this.

1-2-3 will prompt: Enter range to move TO:

Now move the block to the range starting A10.

Press `↓` to A10 and then `ENTER`

The whole range has been shifted down. 1-2-3 will remember the shape and size of the range so you only need to tell it the top left corner (in this case A10). Move the pointer around the range and note how the formulae have been adjusted to reflect their new locations.

Keep practising the COPY and MOVE features.

---

**Key words**          Copy
                       Move

## Task 6 A worked example of a spreadsheet

**Objectives**

To learn how to:
- widen a column
- copy data and formula
- use the @SUM function
- justify a range of labels
- insert or delete a row or column
- use the repeat key

**Instructions**

This task covers a number of different features which appear elsewhere in the Training Guide. Its main aim is to get you to set up a 'real' spreadsheet and to revise some of the work that you have done so far.

You should now be able to create a new spreadsheet looking something like the one on p. 13. Clearly the text and some of the figures will have to be typed in, but if the spreadsheet is to have any advantages over the word processor, you must be able to do better than type the lot in!

---

**Activity 6.1**

Data entry

Type in a company name heading e.g. **Sue, Grabbit and Run** (your name will do). Type all the labels (the text bits), putting Q1 into B3, Q2 into C3 etc. In A5 enter **Sales Income** and move down to enter the other labels — **Cost of sales** in A6, **Gross Profit** in A7 etc. Ignore the dotted lines for now.

On rows 5 and 6, enter the eight sales and cost figures (not the annual totals!)

Note that some of the text in column A is chopped off when you enter figures in B5 and B6. This is because the standard column width is 9 characters.

---

**Activity 6.2**

Widening a column

In column A, press █**W**(orksheet) **C**(olumn) **S**(et-width) and ➡ (arrow right) until all the text reappears in the cell. Press **ENTER**. Instead of using the arrow keys you can type the column width that you require — say 13 in this case. Try both.

Given that the overheads are 15% of sales, all of the remaining empty cells can be filled in by calculation i.e. by 1-2-3 itself. You simply have to tell it what the calculations are.

For example, Gross profit for Quarter 1 (Q1) is Sales less costs. Type **+B5-B6** into B7

| **Activity 6.3** | Copying |
|---|---|

**Activity 6.3** Copying

For the other quarters you will now COPY this formula across.

With the cell pointer in B7 Press **/C**(opy)

The control panel will show the message: Enter range to copy FROM: B7 . . B7

This is the cell you wish to copy so press ENTER

The message will now read: Enter range to copy TO: B7

Type **C7 . . E7** (i.e. Q2 to Q4 Gross Profits) and ENTER

Overheads are 15% of sales so with the cell pointer in B8

Type **+B5*0.15** ENTER

Now copy this formula into C8, D8 and E8. This time copy by pointing rather than typing.

With the cell pointer in B8 Press **/C**(opy)

Read and accept the control panel message by pressing ENTER

Enter range to copy TO:

Move the cell pointer to cell C8 using →

Press . (full stop) to anchor the beginning of the range.

Move → →

Cells C8 to E8 will be highlighted. The control panel will confirm the target range.

Accept by pressing ENTER

This is a good way of copying small ranges of data as you can see what you are getting.

Work out the net profit for Q1 and copy it across as above.

In cell B9 enter **+B7-B8**

**/C**(opy) FROM B9 TO C9 . . E9

---

**Activity 6.4** The @SUM Function

Year totals are best done using one of 1-2-3's many in-built FUNCTIONS.

In cell F5 type @**SUM(B5 . . E5)** ENTER This saves typing +B5+C5 etc.

COPY this formula downwards, this time into F6..F9.

---

**Activity 6.5** Label alignment

The quarterly labels Q1 etc are all left justified and would look better if they were right-aligned with the numbers.

Move to B3 and press **/R**(ange) **L**(abel) **R**(ight).

Use the → key to highlight your labels in row 3, i.e. B3 to F3.

Press ENTER

**Activity 6.6**

Inserting and deleting columns and rows
Finally you need to insert the dotted lines.
Move to row 7 and press **/W**(orksheet) **I**(nsert) **R**(ow) `ENTER`
Move to B7 and Type `\` `–` (backslash key followed by a dash).
The REPEAT key (backslash) will fill the cell with the chosen character.
Copy B7 across to F7 in the usual way.
Insert new rows and create the other two dotted lines as above.
`\` `=` will give you the double-dotted line effect on the last line.
You can insert a new column in much the same way.
Position your cell pointer in column B.
Press **/W**(orksheet) **I**(nsert) **C**(olumn) `ENTER`
A new column B will appear.
Now delete it for practise.
Press **/W**(orksheet **D**(elete) **C**(olumn) `ENTER`
Finally save your work.
**/F**(ile) **S**(ave) and name it `SGR` (or your initials).
Your spreadsheet should look like the following.

|    | A             | B      | C      | D      | E      | F      | G |
|----|---------------|--------|--------|--------|--------|--------|---|
| 1  |               |     SUE,GRABBIT  and RUN |  |      |        |        |   |
| 2  |               |        |        |        |        |        |   |
| 3  |               | Q1     | Q2     | Q3     | Q4     | YEAR   |   |
| 4  |               |        |        |        |        |        |   |
| 5  | Sales income  | 100000 | 120000 | 150000 | 170000 | 540000 |   |
| 6  | Cost of sales | 60000  | 70000  | 90000  | 100000 | 320000 |   |
| 7  |               | ------ | ------ | ------ | ------ | ------ |   |
| 8  | Gross Profit  | 40000  | 50000  | 60000  | 70000  | 220000 |   |
| 9  | Overheads     | 15000  | 18000  | 22500  | 25500  | 81000  |   |
| 10 |               | ------ | ------ | ------ | ------ | ------ |   |
| 11 | Net Profit    | 25000  | 32000  | 37500  | 44500  | 139000 |   |
| 12 |               | ====== | ====== | ====== | ====== | ====== |   |
| 13 |               |        |        |        |        |        |   |
| 14 |               |        |        |        |        |        |   |
| 15 |               |        |        |        |        |        |   |
| 16 |               |        |        |        |        |        |   |
| 17 |               |        |        |        |        |        |   |
| 18 |               |        |        |        |        |        |   |
| 19 |               |        |        |        |        |        |   |
| 20 |               |        |        |        |        |        |   |

| Key words | Copy |
|-----------|------|
|           | @SUM |

13

# Task 7     **Ranges**

**Objectives**

To understand the concept of ranges
To erase a range and create a named range

**Instructions**

Defining ranges
A **range** is a cell or any rectangular block of linked cells. You can tell 1-2-3 what data you want to work with by defining or naming the range.
The following diagram shows a number of ranges.

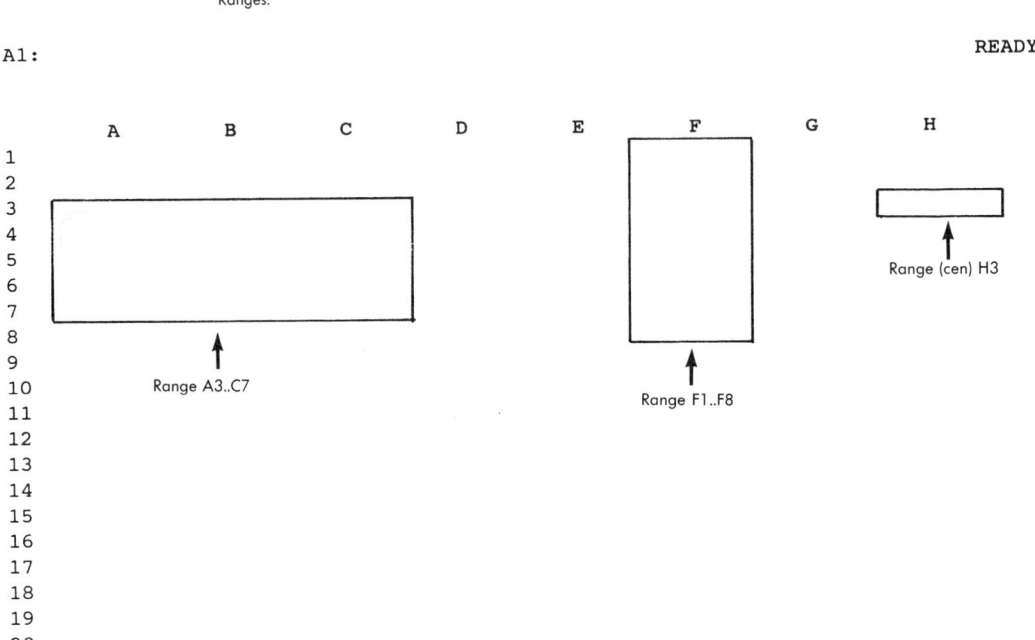

To specify a range you need to indicate the top left and bottom right cell address of the range separated by two full stops.

The range addresses in the diagram are A3 .. C7
                                          F1 .. F8
                                          H3

**Non-contiguous** ranges can also be handled by 1-2-3.
e.g. @SUM(A3 .. C7,F1 .. F8) would sum all the values in these 2 ranges.
You are going to change the quarterly labels and YEAR label and name the range.

| | |
|---|---|
| **Activity 7.1** | Select **/** **F**(ile) **R**(etrieve) **SGR** to call up the Sue, Grabbit and Run file (or the name that you gave the file). |
| | Move to cell B3. |
| | Select **/** **R**(ange) **E**(rase). |
| | Highlight B3 . . F3 with the → key and press **ENTER** |
| | In B3 type **Jan** (press → after each entry to move to the next cell). |
| | In C3 type **Feb** |
| | In D3 type **March** |
| | In E3 type **April** |
| | In F3 type **YTD** (i.e. Year To Date) |

| | |
|---|---|
| **Activity 7.2** | Naming ranges |
| | Naming a range of cells makes life much easier. |
| | Select **/** **R**(ange) **N**(ame) **C**(reate). 1-2-3 will prompt to Enter name: |
| | Type **DATES** **ENTER**. 1-2-3 will prompt to Enter Range: |
| | Highlight B3 . . F3 with the arrow key and press **ENTER** |
| | You should be in F3. This does not matter. You can press the left arrow to B4 to give you the same range. However, if the cell pointer is ever anchored in the wrong cell press **ESC** to unanchor it. |
| | Move to the start (or end) of the range and type . (full stop) to anchor it again. You can then use the pointer keys to highlight the cell range and press **ENTER** |
| | Although nothing has changed on screen you now have a range called DATES which covers cells B3..F3. |
| | You can use this name with **any** command that prompts for a range. |
| | Names should be quicker to use and easier to remember than cell references! |
| | For example, select **/** **R**(ange) **L**(abel) **R**(ight). 1-2-3 will prompt: Enter range of labels: |
| | Type **DATES** (upper or lower case will do) and press **ENTER** |
| | All of the labels in B3 . . F3 should now be right-aligned. Save your file and call it **SGR2** (or choose another name) — you will need to type the file name as it is new. |

| | |
|---|---|
| **Key words** | Range |

# Task 8

## Changing the date-and-time indicator

The date-and-time indicator appears on the status line at the bottom-left of your screen. It is possible to change this to show the name of the file that you are working on. This is useful when you have a large number of files.

**Activity**

Select **/F**(ile) **R**(etrieve) **SGR** to recall the SGR file.

Select **/W**(orksheet) **G**(lobal). The worksheet settings sheet will appear.

Select **D**(efault). The default settings sheet will appear. Note that the clock display setting is standard (bottom right of sheet).

Select **O**(ther) **C**(lock) **F**(ilename). Note that the clock display setting now reads filename and the status line shows SGR.WK1

Select **U**(pdate) **Q**(uit) to save the new setting and return to ready mode.

Now change back to the date-and-time!

Select **/WGDOCCUQ** (just the first letters of the commands shown here!)

# Task 9 — **Formatting the worksheet**

**Objectives**

To show how changes can be made to the appearance of the worksheet and how data is displayed.

**Instructions**

Changing cell formats
1-2-3 lets you display cells in a number of ways. You can use one format for the whole spreadsheet with **/W**(orksheet) **G**(lobal) **F**(ormat) or several different ones by using **/R**(ange) **F**(ormat).

---

**Activity**

Select **/FR** to retrieve the SGR2 file.
You are now going to display all of the numbers with two decimal places.
Select **/WGF F**(ixed) 1-2-3 will prompt:
Enter the number of decimal places:2
Press **ENTER** to accept 2 (the default number).
Asterisks will now show in the cells which are not wide enough to display this format.
Now change the width of all the columns.
Select **/W**(orksheet) **G**(lobal) **C**(olumn-width).
1-2-3 will prompt: Enter global column width (1..240).
Press **→** to increase the width to 10. All of the figures should now be in view.
Press **ENTER** to accept this width.
Try resetting the format to Currency which shows £ signs and commas. You will need to widen the columns again to see the effect.
Select **/WGF C**(urrency) **2** **ENTER**
Select **/WGC 12** (i.e. columns should be set to 12 characters wide)
Now display the Net profit figures in currency as whole numbers.
Select **/R**(ange) **F**(ormat) **C**(urrency) **0** (i.e. no decimal places).
1-2-3 will prompt for the range to format.
Type (or point) **B11 . . E11** **ENTER**
Do not bother to save this file. If you have finished the Task just **/Q**(uit) **Y**(es).

---

| Key words | Format |
|-----------|--------|

# Task 10

## Formatting figures

**Objectives**

To format and present figures
To use Data Fill
To freeze titles on screen

**Instructions**

Presentation of figures

**Input**

Apart from simple numbers you may end a number with a % sign and 1-2-3 will store the entry after dividing it by 100. Thus 15% is stored as 0.15. If necessary, you can also enter numbers in scientific notation; e.g. 1,234,000 as 1.234E+06 (exponential).

**Output**

You learnt in the last task that there are two command sequences for output formats. These are:

**/W**(orksheet) **G**(lobal) **F**(ormat) which lets you set a format for all the cells.

**/R**(ange) **F**(ormat) to control the display in specified ranges.

Either way will display the following menu:

---

*Fixed Sci Currency, General* **+** **/** **—** *Percent Date Text Hidden Reset (/RF only).*
Selection allows you to set the form in which the numbers are presented.

| | |
|---|---|
| Fixed | — specifies number of decimal places |
| Sci(entific) | — number in the form 1.234E+06 |
| Currency | — commas to separate thousands, preceeding £ sign and negative values in brackets e.g. (£234,567.10) |
| Comma (,) | — commas to separate thousands |
| General | — the default format, number usually as input but insignificant zeros to the right of the decimal point are suppressed |
| +/— | — crude bar chart of + or — within cell |
| Percent | — multiplies stored value by 100 and displays it with a % sign |
| Date | — date and time formats — see below |
| Text | — displays formula underlying the number normally shown |
| Hidden | — hides cell contents |
| Reset | — will change specified range of cells to global format |

Try them out in the following activity to see what they do; the right format can give a professional look to a report.

---

**Activity 10.1**  In cells A2 to A11 type in the labels **FIXED**, **SCI** etc just as in the spreadsheet on p. 20.

Now format each of the rows 2 to 11 to match the labels you have just entered.

Move to B2

Type `/RFF 2` `ENTER`

When asked for the range, press `→` `→` `→` `→` `→` `→` (right arrow 6 times) to highlight cells B2 .. H2 then press `ENTER`

This will format row 2 with a fixed format of 2 decimal places.

You can format the other rows yourself now.

Start each row with the cell pointer in column B.

Type `/RF` followed by the initial letter of the relevant format etc.

Note that for COMMA you will need to press the comma key and for DATE choose format 1.

---

**Activity 10.2**  Using Data Fill

Now that you have a block of appropriately formatted cells, insert some numbers using Data Fill.

Move to B1.

Type `/`**D**(ata) **F**(ill).

When asked for the fill range, press . (full stop) to anchor, and `↓` (down arrow) to highlight down to B11 and then press `ENTER`

You will be asked for a start value, so type **7** `ENTER`

Now select the step size, **0** (zero) `ENTER` and finally the upper limit which is already big enough so just press `ENTER`

One or two cells may be full of asterisks which means that they are not wide enough for the display format.

Select `/`**WGC12** to widen all columns to 12 characters.

Now move to C1

Type `/`**DF** and the cursor will move back to column B.

Press `ESC`

Press `→` (right arrow) to C1, . (full stop) to anchor it and point to C11, then press `ENTER`

At the prompt: Start from? try @**TODAY** `ENTER` The step size is still 0 so press `ENTER` and type in **35000** for the ending value then press `ENTER` again.

Note: dates will be explained in greater detail in a later Task.

Now try `/` **D**ata **F**(ill) with some of your own numbers. Try a small decimal like **0.000000123**, or @**DATE** with your birthday in it for example. Try reformatting a cell with more decimal places than you used before.

The FORMAT spreadsheet on p. 20 shows, in cells B1 to F7, how 7, @TODAY, 0.000000123, 37.5 and 12345 look in their various formats!

|    | A | B | C | D | E | F |
|----|---|---|---|---|---|---|
| 1  |         | 7        | 33138        | 0.000000123 | 37.5      | 12345        |
| 2  | FIXED   | 7.00     | 33138.00     | 0.00        | 37.50     | 12345.00     |
| 3  | SCIENTIFIC | 7.00E+00 | 3.31E+04  | 1.23E-07    | 3.75E+01  | 1.23E+04     |
| 4  | CURRENCY | £7.00   | £33,138.00   | £0.00       | £37.50    | £12,345.00   |
| 5  | COMMA   | 7.00     | 33,138.00    | 0.00        | 37.50     | 12,345.00    |
| 6  | GENERAL | 7        | 33138        | 0.000000123 | 37.5      | 12345        |
| 7  | +/-     | ++++++   | ************ . |           | ************************ |  |
| 8  | PERCENT | 700.00%  | 3313800.00%  | 0.00%       | 3750.00%  | 1234500.00%  |
| 9  | DATE    | 07-Jan-00 | 22-Sep-90   | 00-Jan-00   | 06-Feb-00 | 18-Oct-33    |
| 10 | TEXT    | 7        | 33138        | 0.000000123 | 37.5      | 12345        |
| 11 | HIDDEN  |          |              |             |           |              |
| 12 |         |          |              |             |           |              |

---

**Activity 10.3**

Freezing titles on screen

By the time you have reached column G you may have lost column A on your screen. It is useful to see your labels so 'freeze' them.

Move to column B.

Select **/W**(orksheet) **T**(itles) **V**(ertical) to freeze the column to the left of the cell pointer. Try to move to column A; 123 will not let you.

Now move to columns G and H. Note how the labels in column A stay on screen.

Select **/W**(orksheet) **T**(itles) **C**(lear) to 'unfreeze' column A.

---

**Key words**

Data Fill
'Freeze'

## Task 11    **Entering statistics**

**Objectives**    To set up a worksheet involving some of 1-2-3's statistical functions
To revise tasks learnt so far

**Instructions**    Enter the 1-2-3 access system and go into 1-2-3.
Look at the CARS worksheet at the end of this task to see what you are aiming for.
Think about how to lay out the information and, in particular which of the figures are
**derived** i.e. those that you can get 1-2-3 to work out for you.

---

**Activity 11.1**

Move the pointer to C1
Type **Arthur Daley Motors** ENTER
Move to C2 and type **Car sales for August 19-9**
Remember the BACK SPACE key for deleting a character while creating a cell entry
or, once entered, the edit key F2 for changing contents.

| In cell: | Type: | Press: |
|---|---|---|
| B4 | ″**Basic** | → |
| C4 | ″**Special** | → |
| D4 | ″**GTX** | → |
| E4 | ″**Turbo** | → |
| F4 | ″**Deluxe** | Enter |

Press F5 (the goto key) and type **A6**
Then type in the remaining text down the left hand column as follows:

| In cell: | Type: | Press: |
|---|---|---|
| A6 | **Basic Price** | down arrow |
| A7 | **VAT** | ↓ |
| A8 | **Price inc tax** | ↓ |
| A9 | **Number plates** | ↓ |
| A10 | **Price on road** | ↓ ↓ |
| A12 | **Monthly sales** | ↓ |
| A13 | **Total sales** | ↓ ↓ ↓ |
| A16 | **Grand Total** | ↓ ↓ |
| A18 | **Average price** | ↓ |
| A19 | **Number of models** | ↓ |
| A20 | **Best seller (value)** | ↓ |
| A21 | **Worst seller (value)** | ↓ |

Having entered these details you will notice that column A is a bit tight if you are to
enter figures into column B.
To widen the column Press **/** (to call up the commands) and then enter the following
sequence (point or press first letter):
**WCS** (Worksheet, Column, Set-width) and then use the → key to widen the column
(20 characters will do).
Press F5 (function key 5) and move to B6.
Enter the basic prices of the cars as whole numbers in cells B6 to F6 (*see* the CARS
worksheet at the end of the Task for details).

**Activity 11.2**   You are now going to change all the figures to two decimal places so that you can deal in money!
Enter the following command sequence:
**/WGFF** (Worksheet, Global, Format, Fixed) and press **ENTER** to accept the default of two places.
Press **F5** and goto B7.
Type in this formula: **+B6*.15** (i.e. VAT is 15% of basic price)
Now copy this formula across.
Press **/C** (Copy).
The control panel will prompt: Enter range to copy FROM B7 . . B7 Accept by pressing **ENTER**
The copy TO range will appear. Move to the start of the target range by pressing **→** (so that you are in C7). Anchor this cell by pressing . (full stop). Now press **→** **→** **→** to cover (highlight) the area that you want to copy to i.e. C7 . . F7
Press **ENTER**
The VAT figures will now appear. Move the cursor along row 7 and look at each formula in the control panel (top left of display screen). You will see that 1-2-3 has adjusted the formula according to its relative position on the worksheet. **Relative copying** was discussed in Task 4.
Move to B8 and type **+B6+B7**
Copy this across to C8 . . F8.
In B9 type **25** and copy that into C9 . . F9.
In B10 enter **+B8+B9** and copy this along to C10 . . F10.
The top part of your spreadsheet should now be complete — check it with the CARS worksheet at the end of this task. Well done if it agrees; if not go back and check your work.

**Activity 11.3**   Type the monthly sales figures into B12 to F12. All your figures are to two decimal places but you are selling whole cars. You therefore need a range command.
Select **/RFF** (Range, Format, Fixed) and type **0** for the number of decimal places.
Press **ENTER** and the message: Enter range to format will appear.
Type (or point) **B12 . . F12** Your figures in this range should now be whole numbers.
In B13 enter **+B10*B12** and copy across.
In B16 you need to enter the sum of B13 to F13. It is quite legitimate to type **+B13+B14** etc but there is a quicker way and that is by using one of the many functions available in 1-2-3. In B16 Type **@SUM(B13 . . F13)**
You will see a row of asterisks. 1-2-3 is telling you that it has a figure that will not quite fit so widen the column to 10 characters wide.
In B18 type **+B16/@SUM(B12 . . F12)** This formula will divide total sales by the number of cars to find the average selling price.
In B19 type **@COUNT(B4 . . F4)** This function will count the number of types of car sold, (i.e. 5). Reformat the cell to show a whole number.
In B20 type **@MAX(B13 . . F13).** This should pick up the MAXimum sales value in row 13.
Similarly, in B21 type **@MIN(B13 . . F13)** This should give you the MINimum value from the same range.

Obviously these functions are more useful when you have more figures to search for but these should give you the idea.

Now save this worksheet – **/FS** (File Save) with the filename CARS.

Your worksheet should look like the following.

```
filename CARS                    Arthur Daley Motors
                               Car sales for August 19-9

                       Basic    Special      GTX     Turbo    Deluxe

Basic Price            5995.00   6995.00   9995.00  10995.00  15495.00
VAT                     899.25   1049.25   1499.25   1649.25   2324.25
Price inc tax          6894.25   8044.25  11494.25  12644.25  17819.25
Number plates            25.00     25.00     25.00     25.00     25.00
Price on road          6919.25   8069.25  11519.25  12669.25  17844.25

Monthly sales                7        10         6         8         2
Total sales           48434.75  80692.50  69115.50 101354.00  35688.50


Grand Total          335285.25

Average price         10160.16
Number of models             5
Best seller (value)  101354.00
Worst seller "        35688.50
```

# Printing your worksheet

You will want to print out your worksheet at some stage.

Print out the CARS worksheet. Select **▌/FR CARS** if it is not current.

**▌/P**(rint) commands let you create printed copies of a worksheet. Always check that your printer is properly set up and switched on with the paper correctly aligned. You may have to run the INSTALL program again to set up the correct printer drivers.

---

**Activity**

Select **▌/P**(rinter) **R**(ange) then type (or point) **A1 . . F21**

Check the paper and printer status.

Make sure that the print head is at the top of a new sheet of paper.

Select **A**(lign) to tell 1-2-3 that the paper is in position, then select **G** (Go) to start printing.

When printing has finished, select **P**(age) to advance the paper to the top of the next sheet.

Select **Q**(uit).

### Print options

There are many print options including the ability to:

- insert headers and footers at the top and bottom of each page
- set margins - left, right, top or bottom
- set borders - to print column and row references
- set up printer strings - to specify font size and style of print e.g. **▌015** will give compressed print
- determine page length - by specifying the number of lines per page
- print as displayed or the underlying cell formulae, formatted or unformatted

Rather than printing straightaway it is possible to save print files to disk. Files can then be printed out later from DOS or used in other programs such as word processing ones.

Select **▌/P**(rint) **F**(ile) for this routine.

---

**Key words**          Print

## Task 13  Creating graphs

**Objective**  To create graphs from worksheet data

**Instructions**  Graphs are excellent ways of displaying data.
1-2-3 offers 5 types of graph: Line, Bar, XY (scatter graph), Stack-Bar and Pie chart.
You must choose the most appropriate one to show off your data.
You can use data from the CARS worksheet to create a graph.
Select **/FR CARS** worksheet

---

**Activity 13.1**  Creating a bar chart
Select **/G**(raph) **T**(ype) **B**(ar).
Then select **A** for the first data range, (you are going to pick the total sales figures so you only need one data range and A is used in these cases).
At the prompt: Enter first data range: Type (or point) **B13 . . F13**
Select **V**(iew). You will now see the makings of a picture on screen but you still need to add labels etc to explain what it shows.
Press **ESC** to return to the graph menu.
From the Graph menu select **O**(ptions) **T**(itles) **F**(irst). Type in the first line of your graph title – e.g. **Arthur Daley Motors.**
Have a look at your graph again to see the effect, press **ESC** and select **V**(iew).
Now enter the second line of the graph title – from the Graph menu Select **O**(ptions) **T**(itles) **S**(econd) and type **Model sales by value.** Again, **V**(iew) the graph if you wish.
Now you need to label the X and Y axes.
From the Titles menu select **X-Axis**. Type **August 19-9 sales.**
Similarly select the **Y-Axis** and type **£.**
Now label each of the five bar points on the X-axis with the car model names.
From the Graph menu select **X** and type (or point) to the range which covers the five car names – Basic, Special etc i.e. **B4..F4**
Now **V**(iew) your graph. Compare it with the graph on the next page to see if the details are correct.

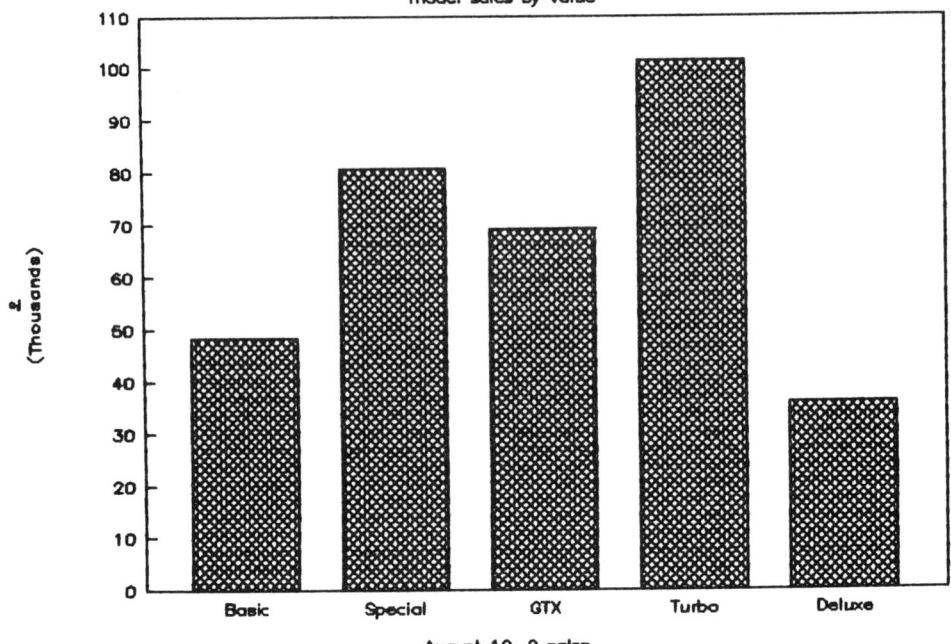

**Arthur Daley Motors**

model sales by value

To save more than one graph with a worksheet you must give each graph a name.
Press `ESC`
From the graph menu Select **N**(ame) **C**(reate)
1-2-3 will prompt: Enter graph name: type **SALES**
This will attach each of the graph settings to the worksheet file.
A graph can change to reflect changes in the worksheet data. Go to your worksheet
and arbitrarily change a figure (e.g. reduce the sales of GTX to 3). Now **V**(iew) the
graph and you will see that it has automatically changed. Graphs are directly
connected to the data that they represent.
To save all this work, press `ESC` `ESC` to get back to the main menu.
Select **/FS** (to accept the filename CARS) and **R**(eplace) the original file. The current
worksheet will look just the same but will now be saved with an underlying graph
attached to it.

**Activity 13.2**      Changing the graph type — a pie chart
Using the same data you can look at the other types of graph. This might help you to decide on the best one to use, for example, a Pie chart.
Select **/G**(raph) **T**(ype) **P**(ie) **V**(iew). A pie chart will appear.
Try out the other types of graph. You will see that the others are not so good for the existing set of data.

Shading pie slices
Although the pie chart looks good, you can improve its appearance with hatch patterns. Return to the spreadsheet `ESC` `ESC`.
1-2-3 has eight hatch patterns numbered 1 to 8 (8 is blank).
Move the pointer to B14 (an empty row).
Select **/D**(ata) **F**(ill)
Enter fill range: **B14 . . F14**
Start: 1 `ENTER` Step: 1 `ENTER` Stop: `ENTER` will accept the default of 8191.
You have now entered 1 2 3 4 and 5 into cells B14..F14 to use with your pie chart.
You could hide these cells with **/** **R**(ange) **F**(ormat) **H**(idden) if, say, you wanted to print the worksheet.
Select **/G**(raph) **T**(ype) **P**(ie) **B** for the second data range.
1-2-3 will prompt: Enter second data range: Type (or point) **B14 . . F14** `ENTER`
Now **V**(iew) the pie chart with hatch patterns.
One further refinement: you can explode one or more slices for emphasis. To do this add 100 to the corresponding hatch pattern.
Press `ESC` until you get back to your worksheet.
Move to F14 and type in **105**
Select **/G**(raph) **V**(iew). Note that the smallest slice has been pulled out (exploded).
Your pie should look like this:

Arthur Daley Motors

model sales by value

Deluxe (10.6%)
Basic (14.4%)
Special (24.1%)
GTX (20.6%)
Turbo (30.2%)

Now save the graph with **/GNC** as above. Call this one PIE.
Save your settings to disk again with **/FS**(ave).

**Activity 13.3**

Multiple data ranges

So far you have just used a single data range showing sales figures.

Now create a graph showing several data ranges – 1-2-3 allows six.

Choose the basic Price, VAT and Price inc Tax figures from the CARS worksheet.

Select **/GT B**(ar)

Select **G**(roup). This is a quick way of nominating a range of data rather than having to define each row (or column) of data separately in data ranges A, B, C etc.

1-2-3 will prompt: Enter group range: Type or point **B4..F8**

Note that this range covers the X data range (the car names) as well as the three rows of figures.

Press **ENTER R**(owwise) to use the rows as data ranges.

Select **V**(iew). Price, VAT and Price inc Tax will be shown in different hatch patterns for each car type.

Press **ESC**

Adding legends

Select **O**(ptions) **L**(egend) **R**(ange).

Move the cell pointer to A5 and highlight A5..A8 then press **ENTER**

Select **Q**(uit) **V**(iew). The graph will now have legends which link the hatch patterns to the data ranges.

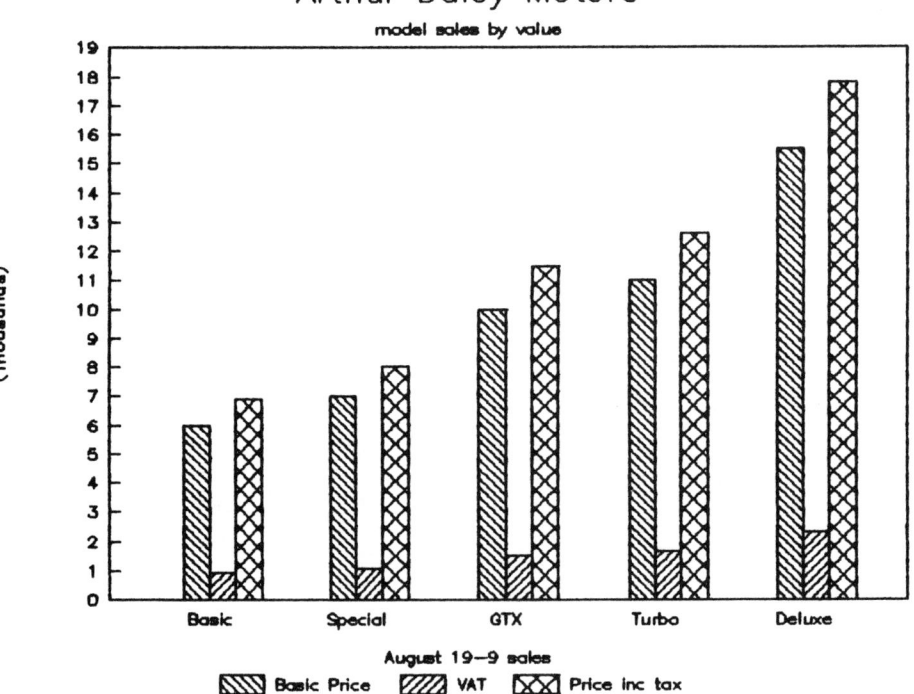

Save the graph by selecting **/GNC** and call it PRICES

Select **/FS** filename CARS to save everything on disk.

Task 14    **Printing graphs**

**Objectives**    To print graphs from worksheet data

**Instructions**    Saving graphs for printing
To save a graph for printing a special .PIC (picture) file has to be created. As 1-2-3 itself does not print graphs, the file will be passed to the PRINTGRAPH or ALLWAYS programs to be printed out.

---

**Activity 14.1**    Print the pie chart in the CARS worksheet.
**/FR** if CARS is not currently in use.
Select **/G**(raph) **N**(ame) **U**(se) and highlight PIE **ENTER**
Press any key to return to the graph menu.
Press **S**(ave) to save the graph and name it PIEPRINT
1-2-3 will automatically add the .PIC extension to show that it is a PICture file. This file is for the PrintGraph program and is static i.e. unlike the graphs attached to the worksheet it does not change if you change the figures.
Repeat the above procedures for your other graphs if you want to print them out too.
In future, you can select **/FLG** (File,List,Graph) to see a list of your .PIC files.
Now that you are back in the worksheet:
Select **/F**(ile) **S**(ave) and accept the filename CARS at the prompt.

---

**Activity 14.2**    The Printgraph program
To print out your graph on paper, leave the 1-2-3 program and start PrintGraph.
Select **/Q**(uit) **Y**(es) to get back to the Access menu.
Select **/P**(rintGraph)
PrintGraph's hardware settings should have been arranged for you but check the following on screen first.
Under Hardware Settings check that your graphs directory is where you have stored your graph (.PIC) files.
If you need to change the setting:
Select **S**(ettings) **H**(ardware) **G**(raphs-Directory) and type in the correct location (e.g. **A:\** if your graphs are on the A drive floppy disk).
Similarly check your fonts directory. This is where the font (.FNT) files are kept and include the typefaces used to print graphs and text. If you need to change the setting:
Select **F**(onts-Directory) (e.g. this would be **C:\** 123 if they were held on a directory called 123 on your hard disk).
Also, check the printer setting. When the program was installed several printers may have been specified so:
Select **P**(rinter).
Use the arrow keys to highlight the printer you wish to use then
Press **SPACE BAR** to mark your selection (a # appears)
Press **ENTER** to accept the printer.
Select **Q**(uit) to return to the settings menu.

If you have made any settings changes:

Select **S**(ave) to save all of these so that you can use them to print graphs in the future.

Now, to print out your hard copy, select **I**(mage-Select). PrintGraph will list all the .PIC files.

Highlight PIE for printing and press `SPACE BAR`. A # sign will appear in front of the filename. This means it has been selected for printing. Press `ENTER`

Adjust the paper and select **A**(lign).

Select **G**(o) to begin printing.

When you have finished, select **P**(age) to advance the paper.

You should now have a printout of a pie chart.

These are the basics for printing graphs. There are many other refinements both within the PrintGraph program and the ALLWAYS publishing add-on which allow you to change scaling, the way numbers are shown, fonts, rotation etc. Although these are beyond the scope of this Training Guide you may wish to experiment.

---

**Activity 14.3**    Try printing the two graphs PIE and PRICES on one page.

Select **S**(ettings) **I**(mage) **S**(ize) **H**(alf) **Q**(uit) three times until you get back to the PrintGraph main menu.

Select **I**(mage-select) and mark the two graphs for printing as above. Press `ENTER`

Select **A**(lign) **G**(o).

Select **P**(age) after printing.

Select **E**(xit) to leave Printgraph.

---

**Key words**    .PIC

PrintGraph

.FNT

# Task 15    **Logical functions**

**Objectives**    To use examples of the @IF, AND, OR and NOT functions

---

**Activity 15.1**

The @IF function

The syntax is:

@**IF**(test, action if true,action if false)

e.g. type an age in years less than 17 into A1

In A2 type @**IF(A1>=17,**"**Ok to drive**",**"Too young**")

This means:

Test: If the figure in A1 is greater than or equal to 17,

then

    (TRUE) display "Ok to drive",

else

    (FALSE) display "Too young"

Now change A1 to any age 17 or over. The test is now true and therefore "Ok to drive" will appear in A2.

---

**Activity 15.2**

AND, OR and NOT functions

These can be used together with the @IF function.

The syntax is:

    AND(Test1, Test2)

    OR(Test1,Test2)

    NOT(Test)

e.g. in A3, A4 and A5 type:

    @**IF(A1>5#AND#A1<10,A1\*3,)**

    i.e. both tests must be TRUE to return A1*3

    @IF(A1=5#OR#B1=7,5,0)

    i.e. either of the tests must be TRUE to return 5.

    @**IF(NOT(A1=7),A1+7,0)**

    i.e. the TRUE result (A1+7) is returned if A1 does NOT contain 7

Experiment by changing the figures in A1 and B1 and looking at the results of these tests.

---

**Key words**    @**IF**

    @**IF(AND)**

    @**IF(OR)**

    @**IF(NOT)**

## Task 16    **Making a date**

**Objectives**

To examine 1-2-3 date functions
To use these functions in formulae
To display dates in different formats

**Instructions**

One of the most useful features of 1-2-3 is its ability to perform arithmetic with dates and to vary their presentation. Each date has a value calculated since 1 January 1900 which is 0. The upper limit is 31 December 2099, 73050 days from the start!
Date functions

| | |
|---|---|
| @**DATE(year,month,day)** | gives the number of days between January 1st 1900 and the date provided. |
| @**TODAY** | does the same but picks up the system date (today's date if set up correctly). |
| @**DAY(number)** | gives the day number in the date. |
| @**MONTH(number)** | gives the month number. |
| @**YEAR(number)** | gives the year number. |

---

**Activity 16.1**

Presentation of dates
The **/R**(ange) **F**(ormat) **D**(ate) option allows you to choose from three ways of converting the strange date numbers above into understandable forms.
You can show dates as: Day-month-year
                             Day-month
                             Month-year
Thus 33089 days since Jan 1st 1900 can be output as 04-Aug-90 or 04-Aug or as Aug-90 (useful for table headings). Try it with **/RFD1** (and then 2 and 3).
As a rule, use functions like @DATE to enter dates into the worksheet and the FORMAT options to control their appearance on screen.

---

**Activity 16.2**

Adding and subtracting dates
Because 1-2-3 stores data in integer form it is easy to determine the number of days between given dates which can be useful in many applications e.g. age, debtor analysis, time, discounts, determining when to trigger reminder letters etc. NWB shares in Task 17 is one such application.
Clear the worksheet screen with **/WE Y**(es).
In A1 type @**TODAY**
In A2 type @**DATE(99,12,25)**
In A3 type +**A2-A1**
The result is the number of days between now and Christmas 1999. A value can be added to or subtracted from a date to produce a new date.
e.g. in A1 type @**TODAY+30**
This will return a number for thirty days hence.
Select **/RFD1** to show the date thirty days from now.
To practice using these functions, create a weekly calendar. Enter start date in cell A1 and use formula **A1+7** and copy down.
Then work out how many days there are between your birthday and Christmas.

| Key words | @DATE |
|---|---|
| | @TODAY |
| | @DAY |
| | @MONTH |
| | @YEAR |

**A worked example using the @DATE function**

**Objectives**

To show more about writing formulae, including dates, and to revise such functions as moving ranges and inserting columns and rows.

**Instructions**

The Northwest Savings Bank
This exercise involves the buying and selling of shares. The spreadsheet below shows what you are aiming to achieve (note the three parts). You will set it up in a slightly different way across the screen so that you can MOVE things around for practise.

```
        A           B           C           D           E           F           G
 1   Northwest Savings Bank <part 1>
 2
 3   Purchase:
 4   =================================================
 5      Date       Shares      Price    Comm(3%)    Cost
 6   -------------------------------------------------
 7   20-Oct-84       100      £0.50      £1.50     £51.50
 8
 9   Sale:  <part 2        >             <      part 3      >
10   =======================================================================
11      Date       Shares      Price    Comm(3%)   Income   gain(loss)   Term
12   -----------------------------------------------------------------------
13   28-Dec-86       100      £0.84      £2.52     £81.48      £29.98    Long
14
15
```

**Activity 17.1**

Buying shares
*See* Part 1 of the spreadsheet.
Start with a blank worksheet and enter a company title (Northwest Savings Bank will do but use any company name if you wish).
Next enter identification labels. Use pointer keys to speed things up.

| *In cell:* | *Enter:* |
|---|---|
| A3 | **Purchase:** |
| A5 | **Date** |
| B5 | **Shares** |
| C5 | **Price** |
| D5 | **Comm(3%)** |
| E5 | **Cost** |

Centre the range of column labels, A5 to E5 by moving to A5 and selecting: **/R**(ange) **L**(abel) **C**(entre).
Highlight the range A5 .. E5 and press ENTER
Next create the double line that separates the column labels from the section heading. Move to A4 and enter \ = (the \ is the repeat key). Then copy to B4 .. E4. Use the same procedure to copy the single line which separates the column labels from the numbers in row 6 (*see* Part 1 again).

**Activity 17.2**

The @ DATE function

Usually the date would be a label but here you want to perform some calculations on it such as how many days between a purchase and a sale. (Can you think of other uses?) To do this you use the @ DATE function.

Enter the share purchase date, 20 October 1984.

Move to cell A7 and type:

@ **DATE (84,10,20)** – i.e. year, month, day. The number 30975 will appear. This is the number of days between January 1 1900 and October 20 1984. @ DATE can convert dates between the years 1900 and 2099.

Date format

Once @ DATE has converted the date to a number it can be displayed in a number of formats. To see the options available select:

**/ R**(ange) **F**(ormat) **D**(ate).

Use the pointer key to read the descriptions.

Accept option **1**, the standard long form, and at the prompt, highlight all the cells in which you want dates to appear (**A7 . . A9** will do for now). Asterisks will appear in A7 indicating that the date will not fit. Widen the column until 20-Oct-84 appears.

Move to B7 and type **100** ENTER – the number of shares purchased

In C7 type **0.50** ENTER The share price is 50 pence

In D7 type +**B7*C7*3%** ENTER

Cell D7 will display 1.5.

Change the format to currency:

Select **/ R**(ange) **F**(ormat) **C**(urrency) **2** ENTER

Format the range C7 . . E9.

Unanchor the pointer with the ESC key. Move to C7. Anchor the pointer with **.**(full stop) and arrow to highlight the range. ENTER

Move to E7 and type +**B7*C7+D7** ENTER

What does this represent? It is the cost of buying shares, i.e. price × number purchased and commission.

---

**Activity 17.3**

Selling shares

*See* Part 2 of the spreadsheet.

Retrieve NWB1. If it is not on screen (use **/ F**(ile) **R**(etrieve) and type or highlight the file name.

Now copy the column labels and lines (A4..E6) to F4. Position this section below the existing one later on.

Move to A4

Select **/** C(opy)

Arrow right four times → → → → and down arrow twice ↓ ↓ to highlight the range. ENTER

Move to F4 ENTER

1-2-3 will copy labels and lines into a new block starting at cell F4.

Note that the active area of your spreadsheet is now larger than the display screen and you must point to see some of your copied labels.

This is a useful time to practise moving around the screen (*see* Task 1).

Move to A4

Press **END** then **→**. This will move the pointer to J4.

Move to A1 (use the **HOME** key) and try **END** **→** again. The pointer has moved to IV1 - the far end of the spreadsheet.

1-2-3 will move in the End-arrow direction until the cell contents change from blank to filled or vice-versa.

Next add the heading 'Sale:' in F3. Use the **F5** Go to key to get there. Move to J5 and change the label from ^ cost to ^ income. Now enter the share sales data.

In F7 enter (in @ DATE format) **28 December 1986.** The number 31774 should appear. To display numbers as dates in column F you will need to format cells F7 . . F9. Try it. 28-Dec-86 should eventually appear in F7 (the asterisks indicate that you need to widen a column to display data).

Type **100** into G7 (i.e. the number of shares sold).

In H7 type 0.84 **ENTER** the selling price per share is 84 pence.

The broker's commission on the share sale is the same formula as used in D7 so try to copy it rather than typing.

2.52 should appear in I7.

Finally, think of a formula in J7 to calculate the amount received from the share sale. If you do not end up with 81.48 in the cell then read the next line!

The formula is: **+G7*H7-I7** i.e. selling price × no of shares less commission. Change the display format of the commission and cost figures to currency.

---

**Activity 17.4**

Moving a range

However much planning you do there is often a need to redesign a worksheet. There are many ways of moving things around. Try the **/M**(ove) command to bring the sales section below the purchase part so that you can see everything on the display screen (you can also print it out as one).

You can name a range and move it but for the purpose of this Task, highlight it this time. Go to F3, select **/M**(ove) and highlight F3 . . J7 at the prompt. Press **ENTER**. Move the section to the area which begins in A9 by moving to cell A9 and pressing **ENTER**. Note again how you only need to tell 1-2-3 where to start the 'TO' range. Press **HOME** to view all your work, then save it as NWB2

---

**Activity 17.5**

Profits (or losses) on share sales

Set up a section to calculate the profit or loss from each completed transaction and determine whether the gain is 'long' or 'short' term. *See* Part 3 of the spreadsheet.

| In cell: | Enter: |
| --- | --- |
| F11 | **^Gain (loss)** |
| G11 | **^Term** |

Extend the double and single lines in rows 10 and 12 into columns F and G using the copy command.

Column F will display gains and losses in amounts up to 5 figures. Set to currency format and widen the column if necessary.

In F13 type **+E13-E7** (i.e. sale − purchase cost).

**Activity 17.6**    The @ IF function
You can compare the dates using 1-2-3's @ IF function.
In G13 type @ **IF(A13-A7>365," Long","Short")**
This means that if the difference between the dates in cells A13 and A7 is greater than 365 days THEN print "Long" ELSE print "Short".
This is the first time that you have used the @ IF function in a serious application. You can see that it can be a very useful tool in spreadsheet work.
In general the syntax for the IF test is:
@**IF** (comparison, result-if-true, result-if-false)
"Long" should appear as a result of the formula.
Now **S**(ave) your worksheet as NWB3.

---

**Activity 17.7**    Entering additional data
*See* Part 4 (on p. 38) of the spreadsheet.
Blank rows or columns can be created to tidy up presentation or to fit extra data.
Now enter data for two more share purchases and sales.
Move to A8 and select **/W**(orksheet) **I**(nsert) **R**(ow) and highlight A8 .. A9.
This will create two blank rows for the new data.
(Use **/W**(orksheet) **D**(elete) to get rid of columns or rows.)
Add the share names in F7 .. F9. Copy them to H15 .. H17 as appropriate.
Make up your own data or use that shown in the spreadsheet.
Cells used should be: A8 to C9 and A16 to C17 (i.e. dates, number of shares and prices only).
You will need to check cell formats and remember that it is quicker and easier to copy formulae.
You can copy more than one formula at a time:
e.g. Range to copy FROM: C7 .. E7
       Range to copy TO: C8 .. E9
Now save your worksheet as NWB4 and print it out.
N.B. You can delete earlier NWB files now if you wish.

---

**Activity 17.8**    Can you see the fatal flaw in the model? You are apparently losing £396.63 on your ROBBER BARON shares.
The model assumes that you always sell **all** the shares in one go and yet you have only sold half of those shares. The model incorrectly shows a heavy loss.
Amend the formula to correct the model.
In F15 type +**E15-(B15*C7*1.03)** and copy down the column to F16 .. F17
In other words, sales income (in E15) minus cost of purchasing same number of shares (quantity in B15, cost in C7 plus 3%).

```
        A           B          C          D          E          F           G
 1  Northwest Savings Bank <part 4>
 2
 3  Purchase:
 4  ===================================================================
 5      Date        Shares      Price    Comm(3%)      Cost      Share name
 6  -------------------------------------------------------------------
 7  20-Oct-84         100      £0.50       £1.50      £51.50  GT Industries
 8  25-Dec-85         500      £1.50      £22.50     £772.50  Robber Baron
 9  20-Oct-84         200      £1.00       £6.00     £206.00  K9P
10
11  Sale:
12  ===================================================================
13      Date        Shares      Price    Comm(3%)     Income    gain(loss)   term
14  -------------------------------------------------------------------
15  28-Dec-86         100      £0.84       £2.52      £81.48       £29.98  Long
16  20-Dec-86         250      £1.55      £11.63     £375.88    (£396.63)  Short
17  03-Jan-91         200      £1.12       £6.72     £217.28       £11.28  Long
18
```

```
        A         B       C        D          E             F          G             H
 1  Northwest Savings Bank - corrected results
 2
 3  Purchase:
 4  =======================================================
 5      Date      Share  Price  Comm(3%)     Cost      Share name
 6  -------------------------------------------------------
 7  20-Oct-84     100   £0.50     £1.50      £51.50  GT Industries
 8  25-Dec-85     500   £1.50    £22.50     £772.50  Robber Baron
 9  20-Oct-84     200   £1.00     £6.00     £206.00  K9P
10
11  Sale:    <part 2      >       <       part 3      >
12  ================================================================
13      Date      Share  Price  Comm(3%)   Income   gain(loss)    term    Share name
14  --------------------------------------------------------------
15  28-Dec-86     100   £0.84     £2.52     £81.48      £29.98   Long    GT Industries
16  20-Dec-86     250   £1.55    £11.63    £375.88    (£10.38)   Short   Robber Baron
17  03-Jan-91     200   £1.12     £6.72    £217.28      £11.28   Long    K9P
18
```

If you want a printout, either select narrow columns with **/WCS** or
select condensed print (set up string **\015** in 1-2-3).

---

| Key words | \ |
| | @DATE |
| | @IF |

# Task 18     **Protecting data and files**

**Objectives**

To protect cells from accidental overwriting
To hide cells from display
To save a file with a password

**Instructions**

It is often sensible to protect or hide all or part of your spreadsheet work. There are many reasons for doing this including confidentiality, the need to prevent changes being made to the formulae in your model or simply to avoid accidental mistakes. You may also want to hide data so that, for example, two non-adjacent columns of work can be printed out alongside each other.

---

**Activity 18.1**

Worksheet (global) protection
Press **/W**(orksheet) **S**(tatus). This shows you, among other things, whether you can protect your work or not.
If Global protection is **Disabled** and you want to prevent changes in your worksheet:
Select **/W**(orksheet) **G**(lobal) **P**(rotection) **E**(nable).
**/WGPD**(isable) will turn protection off again.

---

**Activity 18.2**

Range protection
More commonly you will need to protect cells in a given range.
For example, assume that cells A1 to F8 are your input area where users can enter figures. Assume also that A9 to D20 contain various complicated formulae that you want to protect from accidental change or overwriting.
Press **/R**(ange) **P**(rotect)
Type (or point to) **A9 . . D20**
Move the cell pointer anywhere within the range.
Type 'it will not let me in' `ENTER`
1-2-3 will give a beep and the mode indicator will flash Error.
Press `ESC` to return to READY mode.
**/RU**(nprotected) will cancel protection and allow change when global protection is on.

---

**Activity 18.3**

Hiding data
Type any nine numbers into A1 . . C3. Include a 0 among them.
Select **/R**(ange) **F**(ormat) **H**(idden) **B1 . . B3** — hides cells, in this case the range B1 to B3
**/RFR**(eset) B1..B3 to restore
With the pointer in cell B1:
Select **/W**(orksheet) **C**(olumn) **H**(ide) `ENTER` to hide column B.
**/WCD**(isplay) arrow `←` `ENTER` will bring it back.
**/W**(orksheet) **G**(lobal) **Z**(ero) **Y**(es) will hide all values equal to 0

---

**Activity 18.4**

Saving a file with a password

You can prevent other users from accessing your file by saving it with a password.

1 Retrieve any of your worksheet files using **/FR**.

2 Press **/F**(ile) **S**(ave).

3 Press the `SPACE BAR` once (if the file is new type in the new filename and then press `SPACE BAR`

4 Type **P** and then press `ENTER`

5 1-2-3 will prompt you to enter a password.

6 Type a password up to 15 letters long and press ENTER. Do not forget it!

7 1-2-3 will then ask you to verify the password. Type it in again.

8 Select replace to save your existing file with the password.

9 Now try retrieving the file!

To change a password

1 Select **/FS**(ave)

2 Press `BACKSPACE` to clear the [PASSWORD PROTECTED] prompt.

3 Press `SPACE BAR` and follow the procedure from 4 above.

To delete a password

Follow the instructions for changing a password until:

3 Press `ENTER`

4 Select **R**(eplace) to save the file without a password.

Making a backup copy of a file

It is always sensible to save previous versions of your worksheets.

When you select **/F**(ile) **S**(ave) **B**(ackup) 1-2-3 will create a .BAK (backup file) of the worksheet stored on disk before you write over (i.e. update) the current one with your changes.

---

**Key words**        Protect

# Lookup tables

**Objectives**    To set up a lookup table for referencing

**Instructions**    There are two lookup functions in 1-2-3 – a V (vertical) one for columns and an H (Horizontal) one for rows. As they operate in exactly the same way this Task will examine just the first one.

---

**Activity 19.1**    The @VLOOKUP function

In 1-2-3 the @**VLOOKUP** function can be used to 'look up' a value or code in a table. The first column of the table contains sequential values or letters and the adjacent columns the values or text which are being looked up. The lookup table is set up in a clear area of the spreadsheet but can be viewed on screen with the data if the screen is split into two windows.

e.g. Move to row 12

Select **/W**(orksheet) **W**(indows) **H**(orizontal).

Press function key **F6** to move between the two windows.

Select **/WW C**(lear) to clear the windows and return to the full screen display.

The format for the @VLOOKUP function is:

@**VLOOKUP**(Value, Lookup table range, column offset)

**Value**

This is the value or cell reference holding the value to be looked up. If the value does not match the spreadsheet value then 1-2-3 takes the nearest value rounded down. If the value is smaller than anything in LOOKUP, 1-2-3 returns ERR; anything larger will give the highest value.

**Lookup table range**

This is the range of cells containing the lookup table.

**Column offset**

This is the number of columns from the first column (unfortunately counted as column 0) in the lookup range.

The lookup function is very useful for such applications as tax tables, price lists, exchange rates etc. For example, look at a customer invoice.

Type the following spreadsheet into a new file.

|    | A | B | C | D | E | F | G |
|----|---|---|---|---|---|---|---|
| 1  | PRODUCT: | GO-FASTER RUNNING SHOES | | | | | |
| 2  | PRICE | 29.99 | | | | | |
| 3  | | | | | | | |
| 4  | Customer | Customer | Order | Order | Discount | Invoice | |
| 5  | code | name | Quantity | Value | | Total | |
| 6  | 140 | | 70 | | | | |
| 7  | 150 | | 210 | | | | |
| 8  | 120 | | 35 | | | | |
| 9  | 180 | | 125 | | | | |
| 10 | 160 | | 10 | | | | |
| 11 | 170 | | 175 | | | | |
| 12 | 130 | | 50 | | | | |
| 13 | | | | | | | |
| 14 | | | | | | | |
| 15 | | | | | | | |
| 16 | | | | | | | |
| 17 | | | | | | | |
| 18 | | | | | | | |
| 19 | | | | | | | |
| 20 | | | | | | | |

**Activity 19.2**     Creating and naming LOOKUP tables
You are now going to create two lookup tables to find customer names and then discount amounts.
Type in the following. Again make sure that you use the same cell locations.

|    | A | B | C | D | E | F | G |
|----|---|---|---|---|---|---|---|
| 13 | | | | | | | |
| 14 | LOOKUP TABLES for: | | | | | | |
| 15 | customer name | | | Quantity | Discount rate | | |
| 16 | 120 Alf Tupper | | | 0 | 0.00% | | |
| 17 | 130 Lee Evans | | | 50 | 5.00% | | |
| 18 | 140 Carl Lewis | | | 100 | 10.00% | | |
| 19 | 150 Steve Jones | | | 150 | 15.00% | | |
| 20 | 160 Gordon Jibson | | | 200 | 20.00% | | |
| 21 | 170 Fred Carno | | | | | | |
| 22 | 180 Carlos Lopez | | | | | | |
| 23 | | | | | | | |
| 24 | | | | | | | |
| 25 | | | | | | | |
| 26 | | | | | | | |
| 27 | | | | | | | |
| 28 | | | | | | | |
| 29 | | | | | | | |
| 30 | | | | | | | |
| 31 | | | | | | | |
| 32 | | | | | | | |

Widen column B to accept names longer than 9 characters.
Move to column B.
Select **/WCS 14**
Note that cells E16 to E20 are in Percent Format.
Select **/RFP 2** and highlight this range of cells.
For easier referencing it is advisable to name the lookup tables.
Move to A16.
Select **/RNC** and call it CUSTNAME
Highlight range A16..B22 **ENTER**
Move to D16.
Select **/RNC** and call it DISCOUNT.
Highlight the range D16..E20 **ENTER**

**Activity 19.3**

Using the formulae

In B6 type @**VLOOKUP(A6,$CUSTNAME,1)**

This means the value in A6 (code 140) will be looked up in the CUSTNAME lookup table, column 0. The resulting name found in column 1 will be returned in B6.

Now copy the formula down to B12.

Select **/C**(opy) FROM B6 TO B7..B12

Note that this is another example of MIXED copying i.e. the cell reference for value will change RELATIVE to the spreadsheet position – from A6 to A7 etc, but the reference to the lookup table CUSTNAME will be fixed – so the $ sign will be added – 1-2-3's way of copying ABSOLUTELY.

Move to D6 and type +**$B$2*C6**

i.e. the price (£29.99 in B2) multiplied by the order quantity.

Copy the formula down to D12 as above.

Move to E6 and type @**VLOOKUP(C6,$DISCOUNT,1)*D6**

i.e. check the order quantity in C6 against the lookup table DISCOUNT and return the discount rate.

Copy the formula down to E12 as above.

Move to F6 and type +**D6-E6**

i.e. the invoice total (the amount to bill the customer) is order value minus discount received.

Copy the formula down to F12.

Check all your work with the completed results and formulae below.

|  | A | B | C | D | E | F | G |
|---|---|---|---|---|---|---|---|
| 1 | PRODUCT: | GO-FASTER RUNNING SHOES | | | | | |
| 2 | PRICE | 29.99 | | | | | |
| 3 | | | | | | | |
| 4 | Customer | Customer | Order | Order | Discount | Invoice | |
| 5 | code | name | Quantity | Value | | Total | |
| 6 | 140 | Carl Lewis | 70 | 2099.30 | 104.97 | 1994.34 | |
| 7 | 150 | Steve Jones | 210 | 6297.90 | 1259.58 | 5038.32 | |
| 8 | 120 | Alf Tupper | 35 | 1049.65 | 0.00 | 1049.65 | |
| 9 | 180 | Carlos Lopez | 125 | 3748.75 | 374.88 | 3373.88 | |
| 10 | 160 | Gordon Jibson | 10 | 299.90 | 0.00 | 299.90 | |
| 11 | 170 | Fred Carno | 175 | 5248.25 | 787.24 | 4461.01 | |
| 12 | 130 | Lee Evans | 50 | 1499.50 | 74.98 | 1424.53 | |
| 13 | | | | | | | |

```
PRODUCT: GO-FASTER RUNNING SHOES
PRICE                        29.99

Customer Customer                    Order    Order    Discount                        Invoice
code     name                        Quantity Value                                    Total
    140  @VLOOKUP(A6,$CUSTNAME,1)        70   +$B$2*C6  @VLOOKUP(C6,$DISCOUNT,1)*D6    +D6-E6
    150  @VLOOKUP(A7,$CUSTNAME,1)       210   +$B$2*C7  @VLOOKUP(C7,$DISCOUNT,1)*D7    +D7-E7
    120  @VLOOKUP(A8,$CUSTNAME,1)        35   +$B$2*C8  @VLOOKUP(C8,$DISCOUNT,1)*D8    +D8-E8
    180  @VLOOKUP(A9,$CUSTNAME,1)       125   +$B$2*C9  @VLOOKUP(C9,$DISCOUNT,1)*D9    +D9-E9
    160  @VLOOKUP(A10,$CUSTNAME,1        10   +$B$2*C1  @VLOOKUP(C10,$DISCOUNT,1)*D10  +D10-E10
    170  @VLOOKUP(A11,$CUSTNAME,1       175   +$B$2*C1  @VLOOKUP(C11,$DISCOUNT,1)*D11  +D11-E11
    130  @VLOOKUP(A12,$CUSTNAME,1        50   +$B$2*C1  @VLOOKUP(C12,$DISCOUNT,1)*D12  +D12-E12
```

| **Activity 19.4** | LOOKUPs which require an exact match |
|---|---|
| | If the value or code has to be an exact match, what happens if the wrong code is entered? For example, in the spreadsheet on p. 43 try the following codes in cell A6: 110, 200, 156. They will return ERR (lower than the first code), Carlos Lopez (highest available code) and Steve Jones (nearest code rounded down) respectively. Clearly it is desirable to have an exact match so write the following formula in B6: |
| | **@IF(@VLOOKUP(A6,$CUSTNAME,0)=A6,** |
| | **@VLOOKUP(A6,$CUSTNAME,1),"Wrong code")** |
| | Copy it down to B12. |
| | Now any customer code that does not have an exact match in the CUSTNAME lookup table will return "Wrong code". It can then be reentered correctly. Try it. |
| | Now save the spreadsheet: |
| | Select **/FS** and call it LOOKUP. |

| Key words | @**LOOKUP** |
|---|---|
| | **Value** |
| | **Lookup table range** |
| | **Column offset** |

# Task 20    Linking Files

**Objectives**

To name ranges to make links
To create links between files
To list named ranges in a worksheet
To list target and linked source files

**Instructions**

In this exercise you will look at a shop group. Although it has many shops nationwide, for the purpose of this task you will deal with just two. You will then use data from these source files in a **target file** called LINK which will extract data from both. File linking saves manual updating because *any change to the source files will be reflected automatically in the target file.*

You are going to:

- retrieve worksheet SGR2 (from p. 17, Task 17), add a label and save it as SLOUGH
- change some figures and save it as HULL
- create a target file called LINK.

**Activity 20.1**

Creating source files
Select **/F**(ile) **R**(etrieve) **SGR2** (*see* screen display below)

```
                        SUE,GRABBIT and RUN
                        SLOUGH STORE

                    Jan      Feb     March     April      YTD
Sales income      100000   120000   150000    170000   540000
Cost of sales      60000    70000    90000    100000   320000
                  ---------------------------------------------
Gross Profit       40000    50000    60000     70000   220000
Overheads          15000    18000    22500     25500    81000
                  ---------------------------------------------
Net Profit         25000    32000    37500     44500   139000
                  =============================================

source filename SLOUGH
```

Imagine that this is the profit statement for one shop in a nationwide store chain.
Type the label **SLOUGH STORE** in cell C2.
Name the following ranges in this source file.

1 Move the cell pointer to F5
2 Select **/RNC**
3 Type **YTD-SALES** ENTER and ENTER again to accept range F5.

1 Move to F6
2 Repeat 2 above
3 Type **YTD-COST** ENTER ENTER

1 Move to cell F11
2 Repeat 2 as above
3 Type **YTD-PROFIT** ENTER ENTER

These cells can now be referenced by name in the target file.

Select **/F S**(ave) and save it as SLOUGH.

To save time creating another source file, edit this one for another shop in the chain.

Type **HULL STORE** in cell C2.

Change the following eight sales and cost of sales figures as follows:

| columns | | B | C | D | E |
|---|---|---|---|---|---|
| rows | 5 | 50000 | 20000 | 25000 | 33500 |
| | 6 | 22750 | 35000 | 12340 | 15000 |

Create the range names in this file as for the Slough file i.e.

**YTS-SALES** in F5, **YTD-COST** in F6 and **YTD-PROFIT** in F11.

Select **/FS**(ave) and save the HULL STORE file as HULL.

```
                    SUE,GRABBIT and RUN
                    HULL STORE

                   Jan      Feb    March    April      YTD
  Sales income    50000    20000    25000    33500   128500
  Cost of sales   22750    35000    12340    15000    85090
                 ------------------------------------------
  Gross Profit    27250   -15000    12660    18500    43410
  Overheads        7500     3000     3750     5025    19275
                 ------------------------------------------
  Net Profit      19750   -18000     8910    13475    24135
                 ==========================================

  source filename HULL
```

## Activity 20.2

Creating the target (linked) file

Now set up the target file LINK.

Select **/W E**(rase) **Y**(es) to erase the current worksheet and create the following.

Type in the labels in the appropriate cells following the layout below.

```
        A        B         C         D        E         F        G          H
1
2                SUE, GRABBIT AND RUN
3                COMPANY PROFIT STATEMENT 19-2
4
5                                    ACTUAL              DIFFERENCE
6                YTD       COST OF   NET      % PROFIT   PLANNED  ACTUAL  - PLANNED
7                SALES     SALES     PROFIT   ON SALES   PROFITS  PROFIT
8
9   SLOUGH
10  HULL
11  ------------------------------------------------------------------------------
12  TOTAL
13
14  target filename LINK
15
```

If you enter the right formulae, 1-2-3 will 'pull in' figures for sales, cost of sales and actual net profits from the SLOUGH and HULL source files. You can then create further formulae for the rest.

1 Move to B9

2 Type +<< **SLOUGH**>>**$YTD-SALES**

3 Move to C9

4 Type +<<**SLOUGH**>>**$YTD-COST** Note: it may be quicker to copy the formula in B9 across and edit it.

5 Move to D9

6 Type +<<**SLOUGH**>>**$YTD-PROFIT**

You will see that the figures from the SLOUGH file have appeared.

In cells B10, C10 and D10, repeat the procedure 1 - 6 for the HULL file substituting HULL for SLOUGH

e.g. in B10 you will enter +<<**HULL**>>**$YTD-SALES** and so on.

Now move to E9 Type +**D9/B9** This will divide actual profits by sales.

Select **/R**(ange) **F**(ormat) **P**(ercent) **0** to change the format to %.

Move to F9 Type **125000**

Move to F10 Type **32000** These are head office estimates for the branch profits.

Move to G9 Type +**D9-F9** This is the difference between actual and planned profits.

Move to H9 Type @ **IF(@ ABS(+G9/F9)>15%,"ACTION"," ")**

This long formula means 'If the planned and actual profits differ by more than 15% either way (+ or −) then ACTION should be printed to warn management, otherwise leave blank'.

@**ABS** returns the ABSolute figure without the + or − sign.

This is a good example of EXCEPTION REPORTING. Head Office is apparently concerned with variances + or − 15% in this case.

Select **/C**(opy) and copy the formula FROM E9 . . H9 TO E10 . . H10.

Move to B12.

Type @**SUM(B9.B10)** This will total the shop sales.

**/C**(opy) FROM B12 TO C12..G12 This will add the other figures.

To improve the appearance of cell E12 calculate a crude average.

In E12 Type @**AVG(E9..E10)**

Select **/R**(ange) **F**(ormat) **P**(ercent) **0** to convert to a percentage figure.

Check your final results with the following.


```
SUE, GRABBIT AND RUN
COMPANY PROFIT STATEMENT 19-2
```

| | YTD SALES | COST OF SALES | ACTUAL NET PROFIT | % PROFIT ON SALES | PLANNED PROFITS | DIFFERENCE ACTUAL − PLANNED PROFIT | |
|---|---|---|---|---|---|---|---|
| SLOUGH | 540000 | 320000 | 139000 | 26% | 125000 | 14000 | |
| HULL | 128500 | 85090 | 24135 | 19% | 32000 | -7865 | ACTION |
| TOTAL | 668500 | 405090 | 163135 | 22% | 157000 | 6135 | |

```
target filename LINK
```

Print the file if you wish

Select **/PPR (A1 . . H12) G**

Select **/FS** and call the file LINK.

For your reference, every cell entry is shown below.

```
B2:  'SUE, GRABBIT AND RUN
B3:  'COMPANY PROFIT STATEMENT 19-2
D5:  "ACTUAL
G5:  "DIFFERENCE
B6:  ^YTD
C6:  "COST OF
D6:  '  NET
E6:  "% PROFIT
F6:  "PLANNED
G6:  "ACTUAL - PLANNED
B7:  "SALES
C7:  '  SALES
D7:  "PROFIT
E7:  "ON SALES
F7:  "PROFITS
G7:  'PROFIT
A9:  'SLOUGH
B9:  +<<SLOUGH.WK1>>$YTD-SALES
C9:  +<<SLOUGH.WK1>>$YTD-COST
D9:  +<<SLOUGH.WK1>>$YTD-PROFIT
E9:  (P0) +D9/B9
F9:  125000
G9:  +D9-F9
H9:  @IF(@ABS(+G9/F9)>0.15,"ACTION"," ")
A10: 'HULL
B10: +<<HULL.WK1>>$YTD-SALES
C10: +<<HULL.WK1>>$YTD-COST
D10: +<<HULL.WK1>>$YTD-PROFIT
E10: (P0) +D10/B10
F10: 32000
G10: +D10-F10
H10: @IF(@ABS(+G10/F10)>0.15,"ACTION"," ")
A11: \-
B11: \-
C11: \-
D11: \-
E11: \-
F11: \-
G11: \-
A12: 'TOTAL
B12: @SUM(B9..B10)
C12: @SUM(C9..C10)
D12: @SUM(D9..D10)
E12: (P0) @AVG(E9..E10)
F12: @SUM(F9..F10)
G12: @SUM(G9..G10)
A14: 'target filename LINK
```

---

**Activity 20.3**

The acid test

Now retrieve the SLOUGH file. Press **/FR SLOUGH**

Change the January sales figure to **40000** and save the file.

Now call up the LINK file.

You will see that the figures from SLOUGH have been automatically updated.

To display a list of linked files, select **/F(ile) L(ist) L(inked)**.

Use the arrow keys to see the information for each linked file.

Press **ENTER** to return to ready mode.

---

**Key words**     **LINK**
               **Target File**

# Task 21    **Using a 1-2-3 database**

**Objectives**      To set up and sort a database in 1-2-3

**Instructions**    1-2-3 allows you to set up and use simple databases arranged by rows and columns. Set up the sample staff database in the format shown below.

STAFF DATABASE

| EMPNO | FIRSTNAME | SURNAME | SEX | SALARY | DEPARTMENT | DOB ◄——fieldname |
|-------|-----------|---------|-----|--------|------------|-----|
| 1 | CHRIS | WADDLE | M | 16000 | ACCOUNTS | 20-Oct-53 |
| 2 | PAUL | GASCOINE | M | 18500 | PERSONNEL | 18-Jul-63 |
| 3 | ANNE | SUTTLE | F | 20000 | MARKETING | 15-Dec-56 ◄—record |
| 4 | JOHN | FINCH | M | 25000 | PURCHASING | 03-Mar-50 |
| 5 | DAVE | SHEARGOLD | M | 30000 | MARKETING | 29-Mar-47 |
| 6 | BOB | LOMAS | M | 18250 | ACCOUNTS | 25-Dec-63 ◄—field |
| 7 | MARGARET | OWEN | F | 21750 | PERSONNEL | 20-Oct-60 |
| 8 | JUDY | CASSELLS | F | 12500 | PURCHASING | 21-Mar-34 |
| 9 | ILENE | DOVER | F | 14000 | ACCOUNTS | 20-Oct-53 |
| 10 | ALAN | WAINWRIGHT | M | 9500 | ACCOUNTS | 07-Feb-68 |
| 11 | GILLIAN | WHITEHEAD | F | 15500 | MARKETING | 06-Mar-55 |
| 12 | DOUG | TAYLOR | M | 23500 | PERSONNEL | 16-Aug-53 |
| 13 | DES | WALKER | M | 27500 | ACCOUNTS | 02-Jan-65 |
| 14 | DEL | AMITRI | F | 19750 | MARKETING | 18-Nov-63 |
| 15 | PETER | GABRIEL | M | 22000 | PERSONNEL | 20-Dec-49 |
| 16 | ANDY | TOPLIS | M | 9500 | ACCOUNTS | 17-Nov-47 |
| 17 | JURGEN | KLINSMAN | M | 12500 | PERSONNEL | 04-Mar-66 |
| 18 | GLADYS | HEYWOOD | F | 16000 | PURCHASING | 10-Oct-53 |
| 19 | GRAHAM | GREEN | M | 35000 | MARKETING | 07-Feb-68 |
| 20 | KIM | BASINGER | F | 14500 | ACCOUNTS | 06-Jun-55 |

Note that there are 20 **records** each containing 7 **fields**.
**Field names** are the labels at the top of each column in row 3.
Database rules
- Field names must be in the first row, records follow.
- No blank rows or dotted divider lines are permitted.
- A field name must be a label and entered in a single cell. Use something which identifies the data held in the field. The sample database fieldnames are self-explanatory except for the two abbreviated ones: EMPNO = Employer Number; DOB = Date of Birth.
- Data entries in the field must be all text (labels) or all numbers (values) not both.
- A 1-2-3 database can contain up to 256 fields and 8191 records
Practise moving around the database using the pointer movement keys. This is important as your databases get bigger.

---

**Activity 21.1**    Sorting a database
You can see that the records are currently ordered by employee number. (N.B. Did you use **/D**(ata) **F**(ill) to create this column?)
You are now going to sort the records alphabetically by last name.
This involves specifying a:
- range to sort
- field(s) to sort by
- sort order.

Select **/D**(ata) **S**(ort) and a settings sheet will appear.
Select **D**(ata-Range) and highlight all of the records and fields in the database by pointing to or typing the cell range **A4** to **G27**.
The settings sheet will display this.
N.B. You do *not* wish to sort the field names!
Select **P**(rimary-key) and move to any cell in the SURNAME field and **ENTER**
Select **A** for Ascending order (A-Z)
Select **G**(o) to sort the records.
The records will now appear in surname order.

---

**Activity 21.2**

Sorting using two keys
Now try to get everyone in alphabetical order by SURNAME but within DEPARTMENT.
Select **/D**(ata) **S**(ort).
The settings sheet will appear again.
You are using the same data range (A4 to G27) so:
Select **P**(rimary-key) and move to any cell in the DEPARTMENT field and press **ENTER**
Select **A** for Ascending order.
Select **S**(econdary-key) and move to any cell in the SURNAME field and **ENTER**.
Type **A** for Ascending order (A-Z).
Select **G**(o) to sort the records.
You should now see all the people in ACCOUNTS in alphabetical order by SURNAME and so on.

---

**Activity 21.3**

Further practise
1 SORT the database by DOB (Date Of Birth) showing the youngest first.
2 SORT the database with Females first in salary order.
3 SORT the database back to its original order (by EMPNO).
Select **/F**(ile) **S**(ave) and save the original file calling it **DATABASE**.
Answers
**/D**(ata) **S**(ort)

|   | *Primary-key* | *Order* | *Secondary-key* | *Order* |
|---|---|---|---|---|
| 1 | DOB | D | | |
| 2 | SEX | A | SALARY | A |
| 3 | EMPNO | A | | |

---

**Key words**

**Sort**
**Primary-key**
**Secondary-key**

# Task 22      Searching a database

**Objectives**

To show how to set up search criteria to find specific records
To extract those records from the database

**Instructions**

You can search for particular records in a database that meet selected criteria. This is invaluable if your database is large.

It is useful to **/F**(reeze) **T**itles if you have a large number of records and fields so that you keep the field names on screen.

You are going to find all of the females in the sample file named DATABASE. Retrieve this file if you have to.

Setting up a query is a five-stage process.

---

**Activity 22.1**

Searching for data

**1 Set up a criteria range**

**/C**(opy) A3.G3 (the field names) into A25 (remember 1-2-3 will remember the range shape).

You have copied all of the field names so that other searches can be easily carried out.

**2 Enter the criteria**

In the cell beneath SEX, i.e. D26, type **F** (you are searching for Females).

```
CRITERIA for finding females (SEX = "F")

EMPNO FIRSTNAME   SURNAME      SEX    SALARY DEPARTMENT     DOB
                               F
```

**3 Specify the criteria range**

Select **/D**(ata) **Q**(uery).

The Data Query settings sheet will appear.

Select **C**(riteria).

Highlight (or type) **A25.G26,** i.e. one row of field names and one row of criteria.

**4 Specify the input range**

This is the database that you wish to search and is similar to the data range you specified for SORTing except that you must include the field names as well as the records.

Select **I**(nput).

Highlight or type **A3.G23**

**5 Find records in the database**

Select **F**(ind).

The first female (Anne Suttle) should be highlighted.

Press ⬇️ (down arrow) for the next one, and so on until the end of the database. 1-2-3 will give an audible beep after the last record found.

Now find all the females earning £15000 or more.

Press **ESC** until you are back in READY mode. Go to cell E26 and type **+E4>=15000**

Cell E26 is just below the SALARY field name in the criteria range. The formula says: Is the salary figure in E4 (the first entry in the database input range) equal to or greater than £15000?

Note that in E26 the figure 1 is shown. This denotes that the result of the test is true (0 is false).

As you have already set up the input and criteria ranges and the SEX = F criteria you can proceed.

Select **D**(ata) **Q**(uery) **F**(ind).

Note that the first female earning £15000 or more (Anne again) is highlighted.

Press ⬇ (down arrow) to see the other records that pass the tests.

---

**Activity 22.2**

Further practise

1 FIND people earning between 15000 *and* 20000.

2 FIND people whose surname begins with G.

3 FIND everyone in either PERSONNEL or MARKETING.

*Answers*

When you have set up the new criteria, select **D**(ata) **Q**(uery) **F**(ind) each time.

1 In cell E26 edit to +E4>=15000£AND£+E4<=20000 (using logical AND)

2 **/R**(ange) **E**(rase) D26..E26 and enter **G*** into C26. The * is a wild card which will match all characters to the end of the label.

3 **/R**(ange) **E**(rase) C26 and enter **PERSONNEL** in cell F26 and **MARKETING** in cell F27.

Redefine the criteria range to include cell F27, i.e. A25..G27, then **/D**(ata) **Q**(uery) **F**(ind).

---

**Activity 22.3**

Extracting records

Sometimes it is useful to show your selected records separately from the database in what is called the **Output area**. These can then be examined on screen or printed out.

Using the input range, criteria and criteria range from the last example you are going to extract all of the people from the PERSONNELdepartment.

Select **/D**(ata) **Q**(uery) **C**(riteria) and amend the range to A25.G26 (chopping off the MARKETING test).

**/C**(opy) the field names (A3.F3) to cell A30.

N.B. You do not have to copy all of the field names and they can be put in any order in the output range e.g. you have left off DOB. Swap FIRSTNAME and SURNAME in B30 and C30 to prove this.

Select **/D**(ata) **Q**(uery) **O**(utput). Define the range A30.F30

If you select a single row for the output range 1-2-3 will take up as many rows as needed to show the extracted records; however, it will erase data that gets in the way so it may be prudent to specify several rows. If the range is too small to fit the extract, 1-2-3 will beep at you with an error message. If this happens press **ESC** and enlarge the output area.

Select **E**(xtract) **Q**(uit) to return to Ready mode.

Move the cell pointer to A30 to see your results. They should look as follows.

```
EXTRACTED file - people in PERSONNEL

EMPNO  SURNAME      FIRSTNAME     SEX     SALARY  DEPARTMENT
    2  GASCOINE     PAUL          M        18500  PERSONNEL
    7  OWEN         MARGARET      F        21750  PERSONNEL
   12  TAYLOR       DOUG          M        23500  PERSONNEL
   15  GABRIEL      PETER         M        22000  PERSONNEL
   17  KLINSMAN     JURGEN        M        12500  PERSONNEL
```

| Key words | Criteria |
|-----------|----------|
|           | Freeze   |
|           | Find     |

## Task 23 — Database statistical functions

**Objectives**

To examine some of 1-2-3's database statistical functions.

**Instructions**

There are seven statistical functions in 1-2-3 that can be used with a database. These are:

@**DAVG** averages values
@**DCOUNT** counts the records
@**DMAX** finds the largest value
@**DSUM** sums values
@**DMIN** finds the smallest value
@**DSTD** calculates standard deviation
@**DVAR** calculates variance

The general format for these functions is as follows:

@**function**(input range, offset number, criteria range)

The input range is the section of the database used in the calculation.
The offset number identifies the field for calculation.
The criteria range is where the selection criteria is found.

---

**Activity 23.1**

Use the more popular functions with the STAFF database. Work out, for the ACCOUNTS department, the average salary, total salary bill, the best paid accountant and the number of employees.

Select **/FR STAFF** to retrieve the STAFF database.

Name the input and criteria ranges as follows:

Move to A3.
Select **/R**(ange) **N**(ame) **C**(reate).
Type **INPUT** ENTER to accept the name.
Highlight A3..G23 ENTER to accept.
Move to A25.
Select **/RNC**
Type **CRITERIA** ENTER
Highlight A25 .. G26

Check the contents of the criteria range. It will probably contain tests from your previous tasks so delete them by pressing **/R**(ange) **E**(rase) A26 .. G27

Move to F26
Type **ACCOUNTS**

You can now use these two named ranges in your formulae.

In A40 type **Average salary in ACCOUNTS department**
In A41 type **Total salary bill in ACCOUNTS**
In A42 type **Best paid accountant**
In A43 type **Number of employees in ACCOUNTS**

Now enter the formulae:

In F40 type @**DAVG(INPUT,4,CRITERIA)**
In F41 type @**DSUM(INPUT,4,CRITERIA)**
In F42 type @**DMAX(INPUT,4,CRITERIA)**
In F43 type @**DCOUNT(INPUT,4,CRITERIA)**

You will need to format the figures.

Move to F40.

Select **/RFC2**
Highlight F40..F42
The overflow in F41 can be overcome by widening the column (**/WGCS12**) or
formatting this cell to currency but with no pence i.e. **/RFC0**
The following spreadsheet should be shown on your screen.

```
Criteria range:

EMPNO FIRSTNAME  SURNAME     SEX    SALARY DEPARTMENT      DOB    ◄─── Criteria
                                           ACCOUNTS


Results:

Average salary in ACCOUNTS department      $15,607.14        ◄─── Results
Total salary bill in ACCOUNTS              $109,250
Best paid accountant                       $27,500.00
Number of employees in ACCOUNTS                     7
```

| Key words | @**DAVG** |
| --- | --- |
| | @**DCOUNT** |
| | @**DMAX** |
| | @**DSUM** |
| | @**DMIN** |
| | @**DSTD** |
| | @**DVAR** |
| | @**Function** |

## Task 24        **Macros**

**Objectives**    To outline macros and their uses
To create a macro to complete cells with standard entries

**Instructions**    You can automate any task in 1-2-3 by creating a macro. A macro is a series of instructions — keystrokes and commands — that can be saved and used over and over again.
Macros are useful for:
- repeated tasks requiring accuracy
- frequently used labels, numbers and formulae
- selecting command sequences
- prompting a user for typing input
- testing cell entries and performing actions based on those entries
- building command menus

There are 4 basic steps to creating a macro:
1 PLANNING - Objectives - Plan what you want to do
2 ENTERING - Type macro instructions into the worksheet
3 EXECUTING - Carry out instructions
4 DEBUGGING - Correct errors

When **planning** the macro you need to decide where to put it and what instructions to write in it.
To **enter** a macro, type your commands in a column of cells leaving a blank cell at the end.
Macro instructions can use one or more rows.
- Breaking up instructions on separate rows makes them easier to read
- Blank rows are not allowed (Blank means end of macro)
- It is conventional to type the macro away from the standard worksheet area.

Writing macro instructions
Use ' to start a macro (or any label prefix - "^)
e.g. '^ 1st Quarter
To move the pointer use braces eg {right}
Tilde ( ~ ) stands for **ENTER**.
Press **ENTER** to move instructions from the command line to the worksheet.
Refer to the 1-2-3 reference book for further macro instructions.

---

**Activity 24.1**    Your first macro example
Enter the following as TEXT. You may also like to type in a brief explanation of what the macro does alongside in a separate column — *see* comments below. Note: these are *not* part of the macro, simply onscreen descriptions.

|  |  | *Comments* |
|---|---|---|
| In cell A2 | **'Selling costs** ~ | enters label |
| A3 | **'/WCS 14** ~ **{right}** | sets column A width to 14 ,moves → |
| A4 | **'/RFC2** ~ | sets column B format to currency with 2 digits |
| A5 | **'100** ~ | enters number |
| A6 | **'{goto}A9** ~ | puts cell pointer at C1 |
| A7 |  | leave as a BLANK CELL |

To name a macro select **/R**(ange) **N**(ame) **C**(reate).
Type **macro1**
Accept the range of the macro (A2..A7 in this case).
Move to A1 and type **macro1** ENTER to show the macro name.

**Activity 24.2**
Executing the macro
Execute (invoke) your macros as follows:
Move to cell A8 — the start cell for your display.
Press ALT+F3 (i.e. hold down the ALT key and press function key F3).
Select the macro to run: **macro1**
The following will appear on your screen.

```
macro1
Selling costs~
/wcs 14~{right}
/rfc2~~
100~
{goto}a9~

Selling costs  $100.00
```

To execute a macro step-by-step press any key after each step and ALT+F2 to
resume normal operation. This process is useful for finding bugs.
To save your macro select **/FS** and the macro will be saved with the worksheet.

**Key words**
Macro
ALT+F2
ALT+F3

## Task 25

# Interactive macros, macros for selecting commands and the macro LEARN feature

**Objectives**
To create interactive macros for entering keyboard data
To create macros for 1-2-3 command sequences
To use 1-2-3's macro LEARN facility

**Instructions**
Accepting input
Interactive macros are useful for creating 'form-filling' routines.
Pausing for, and accepting input requires special macro syntax.
(?) causes macro execution to pause for input.
Tilde (~) – the automatic return – shows that the RETURN key is expected after user-input before the macro execution will resume.

---

**Activity 25.1**

Clear the screen with **/WE Y**(es)
Type in the following macro in column A.

| Macro | Input area |
|---|---|
| `APPLICATION FORM{D}` | `APPLICATION FORM` |
| `{D}` | |
| `Enter name:{R}` | `Enter name:      {?}` |
| `{R}` | |
| `{?}{D}` | `Enter birthdate:  @date({?})` |
| `{D}` | |
| `{L}` | |
| `{L}` | |
| `Enter birthdate:{R}` | |
| `{R}` | |
| `@date({?})~` | |
| `/rfd1~` | |
| `/wcs10~{d}` | |

*Sample result*

```
APPLICATION FORM

Enter name:      fred

Enter birthdate:  12-Dec-55
```

Press **/RNC** and name the macro APPLIC
Press ENTER to accept the range A1 .. A12
Again it may be helpful to have brief explanatory comments on screen alongside the macro and the macro name clearly displayed for reference.
To execute the macro:
Move to cell D1.
Press ALT+F3 and highlight APPLIC
Note that the macro pauses in cell F3.
Type in your name then press ENTER
The cursor moves to **F5** and **@date** will appear in the command line.
Type in your birthday in YYMMDD format e.g. 55,10,08 would give 08-Oct-55.
Select **/FS** to save the macro with the worksheet if you wish.

58

**Activity 25.2**

Selecting commands

Macros can be used for the automatic selection of 1-2-3 command sequences

For example, type in the following in column AA:

In cell AA1 **'/WGFC0** ~ (Worksheet Global Format Currency 0)

In cell AA2 **'/RFC2**{**Esc**}{**End**}{**Left**}.{**End**}{**Right**} ~ Range Format
Currency 2

Select /**RNC** and name it FORMAT. Select range AA1 . . AA2

Enter a few numbers into your worksheet to test it.

Go to A1. Select **/** **D**(ata) **F**(ill).

Enter fill range A1 . . E10 Start:1 Step:1 End **ENTER**

In A1 Press **ALT+F3** to run FORMAT

Note that this macro sets the worksheet format to currency, with no decimal places,
but allows two decimal places on line 2.

Select **/FS** if you wish to save the file.

---

**Activity 25.3**

Set up a macro to split the window horizontally and set the global column width to 6.*

Type into cell:

| | |
|---|---|
| AA1 | **Window macro** |
| AB2 | **'/WWH** ~ | split window horizontally |
| AB3 | **'/WGC6** ~~ | set global column width to 6 |

Press **/RNC** WINDOW and accept range AB2 . . AB3

Goto cell A10

Press **ALT+F3** to execute the macro.

Press **F6** to move between windows.

Select **/W**(orksheet) **W**(indows) **C**(lear) to clear the window setting.

---

**Activity 25.4**

Using the macro learn feature

An easy way to create macros is to get 1-2-3 to record your keystrokes as you do
them so that they can be used again.

This involves 4 steps:

**setting up** a column (the **learn range**) to record your keystrokes

**pressing** **ALT+F5** to turn on LEARN

**entering** your macro

**pressing** **ALT+F5** again to switch off LEARN

You will now create a macro to enter a record company's name and sales headings
as shown below.

```
Heading     r{BS}                          Description:
macro       R.STORNAWAY{D}                 enters company name
            PRODUCT SALES #000s{D}         and product sales
            {D}                            headings
            LPs{R}
            SINGLES{R}
            CDs{D}


            Result:              R.STORNAWAY
                                 PRODUCT SALES #000s

                                 LPs        SINGLES   CDs
```

In A1 type **Heading**

In A2 type **macro**

Select **/W**(orksheet) **L**(earn) **R**(ange) and select B1 .. B7

(Usually you will not know how big your macro will be so use more cells than you think you will need).

Move to B10.

Press `ALT+F5` to turn on LEARN. From now on all of your keystrokes will be recorded.

In B10 type **R STORNAWAY** and press `↓` (down arrow).

In B11 type **PRODUCT SALES £000s** and press `↓` `↓`

In B13 type **LPs** `→`

In C13 type **SINGLES** `↳`

In D13 type **CDs** `↓`

Press `ALT+F5` to finish LEARN and then press `ENTER`

Select **/R**(ange) **E**(rase) B10 .. D13 to erase your input.

Select **/RNC** and call it HEADING

Enter range as B1 .. B7

Move to D10

Press `ALT+F3` and accept HEADING as the macro to execute.

The company headings will appear as specified in the macro at this location.

---

| Key words | |
|---|---|
| | `ALT+F3` |
| | `ALT+F5` |

# Case study: The Hot-Stuff Heating Company

**Objectives**    To bring together and revise all that has been learnt in Tasks 1-25

**The problem:**    Jack Sharpe, sole proprietor of the Hot-Stuff Heating Company, with capital of £6500 in his bank and an anticipated legacy which he will invest in the business, plans to produce and sell a superior gas fire for next winter.

His plans for the business are as follows:

1 He will produce 60 gas-fires a month but expects sales to start from 30 July, increasing in steps of 10 until October and then in steps of 20 in November and December when he reaches 100 per month.

2 The fires will sell for £180 each but his customers' accounts will not be settled until the third month after the month of purchase.

3 His overheads will be £1000 a month, paid one month in arrears.

4 In September he will pay for the £20,000 of equipment, machinery and computers, he is to buy to start up the business.

5 In November, his solicitor has advised him, he should receive a legacy of £30,000 from the Brazilian estate of his long lost uncle.

6 His unit production costs, which it is not anticipated will rise in the period under review, will be as follows:

Materials         £50
Labour         £40
Variables       £30

7 He will buy materials as needed, paying for them two months later; labour will have to be paid for in the month of production as will his variable costs.

8 Interest charges on the previous month's overdraft will be debited at a rate of 1.5% (one and a half percent) per month.

In order to satisfy his bank manager that his request for a £20,000 overdraft facility will be sufficient to meet the needs of his enterprise in its start-up phase, he needs to draw up a cash-flow forecast for the first six months of operations: that is, from July until December.

---

**Activity 26.1**    Use LOTUS 1-2-3 to create the cash-flow table that Jack's bank manager will want to see before granting him the overdraft facility he has asked for. A suggested format for the cashflow forecast is shown on page 62.

You should produce not only the print of the table as seen on the screen but also, in case the bank manager questions the derivation of the figures, a print showing the underlying formulae used in its production!

```
 1       A              B        C      D      E      F      G
 1  THE HOTSTUFF HEATING COMPANY
 2  Cash Flow Analysis for 19-8
 3  ================================================================
 4                      JUL    AUG    SEP    OCT    NOV    DEC
 5
 6  Cash in Bank
 7  ----------------------------------------------------------------
 8  CASH INFLOW:
 9
10  Sales Volume
11  Unit Price
12
13  Sales Income
14  Legacy
15
16  Sub-total in
17  ----------------------------------------------------------------
18  CASH OUTFLOW:
19
20  Prod'n Volume
21  Unit Costs:
22     materials
23     labour
24     variables
25
26  Total Prod'n Costs
27
28  Fixed O'heads
29  New machinery
30  Overdraft charges
31
32  Sub-total out
33  ----------------------------------------------------------------
34  C/F to Bank
35  ================================================================
```

## The problems of success!

By October Jack Sharpe finds that the business is proceeding very much as he had planned and that advance orders suggest that sales are likely to be maintained at the December level during January and February, falling to 50 or 60 in March. This is extremely encouraging but leaves Jack with the problem of how he is going to be able to satisfy the demand.

His production capacity of 60 gas fires a month has been sufficient in the start-up phase because his stocks have been sufficient to cope with the November/December demand but over the colder months of winter he anticipates that stocks will need to be increased.

Overtime working, which will inevitably increase his labour costs, seems to be called for and Jack starts to think about how this can be organised.

Weekday and Saturday morning overtime will cost him time-and-a-half, Saturday afternoon and Sunday morning, double time. With the employment situation as it is and Christmas on the horizon, his workforce will be glad of the overtime but Jack's problem is how much, when and how this will affect his overdraft.

After his experience with the first cash-flow analysis, Jack has discarded the idea of guessing what his needs will be and has decided that he had better extend the analysis until April. He has accordingly asked you to do some 'what if' analysis for him.

**Activity 26.2**     Use LOTUS 1-2-3 and with your existing model as a starting point, extend the analysis until April and investigate some of the possibilities open to Jack. You may assume that only the labour cost will be affected by the overtime working and should remember that selling machines Jack has not produced is not an acceptable means of improving the cash-flow!

To ensure that you have a record of the consequences of the alternative strategies you have investigated, print copies of the sheets with sub-headings to indicate what strategy you are examining.

# Appendix I

## 1-2-3's functions

This section gives a brief overview of some of the most useful business functions found in LOTUS 1-2-3.

Functions make formulae more powerful. There are more than 50 to choose from and you can only really learn about them and their various applications by trying them out. They can be categorised as follows:

statistical
mathematical
logical
data management
error trapping
date arithmetic
financial
database statistical
string.

**Function syntax**

A function has three parts:

prefix                    – @
name                 – e.g. **AVG**
argument            – e.g. **(C2 . . C7)**

Different functions have different arguments. A few have no argument at all.

e.g.        @**SUM(A1 . . B10)**    – argument is a range
              @**TODAY**                – no argument
              @**IF(A1>0,B1,C1)**    – conditional test followed by two values

**Statistical functions**

There are seven of these:

@**COUNT**      counts the number of items
@**SUM**         adds the values
@**AVG**          finds the average
@**MIN**          identifies the minimum value
@**MAX**         identifies the maximum value
@**STD**          calculates standard deviation
@**VAR**          calculates variance

A list of cells must be specified as the argument. A simple list would just be one cell or range of cells e.g. @**SUM(B2 . . B7).** But you can include more than one cell or range like this:

@**SUM(B2 . . B4,B6 . . B8,B10 . . B12,B15,B20)**

Empty cells are ignored.
Labels will have a value of 0.

**Logical functions**

@**FALSE**                    indicates or returns a value of 0
@**TRUE**                     indicates or returns a value of 1
@**IF**(condition,x,y)       IF condition is true, returns x; if false returns y
@**IF**                        can be used in many ways to produce results based on evaluation of data in other cells.

For example, suppose the number of hours worked was held in cell B2, overtime was paid at time-and-a-half if hours exceeded 40 and the hourly pay rate was in C2. The formula for calculating weekly pay would be: @**IF(B2>=40,(B2-40)\*C2\*1.5+ 40\*C2,B2\*C2)**

@**ISERR(x)** assigns a value of 1 if x is an unacceptable value.
@**ISNA(x)** assigns a value of 1 if x is an unavailable value

## Data management functions

These retrieve data from lists and tables.
@**CHOOSE(x,v0,v1,v2 . . )** chooses the xth value in a list
@**HLOOKUP(x,range,n)** looks up values in horizontal and vertical tables respectively.
@**VLOOKUP(x,range,n)** e.g. @**VLOOKUP(525,A4..E7,3)** uses 525 as the test (lookup) value, A4 . . E7 as the table range and 3 as the offset value i.e. the number of columns along.

## Error trapping functions

These allow you to flag omissions or errors.
@**NA**        means not available
@**ERR**       means error, not acceptable

## Date and time functions

Dates entered as ordinary labels cannot be used directly in formulae or functions as they have *no numeric value*. Hence functions are used that generate serial date and time numbers:
@**DATE(year,month,day)** is used to enter dates; it assigns a numeric value to each date to allow arithmetic operations
@**DATEVALUE(date string)** – the date number of date string
@**NOW** – serial number for current date and time
@**TIME(hr,min,sec)** cf @DATE
@**TIMEVALUE**(time string) cf @DATEVALUE
Functions that use serial date and time numbers:
@**DAY(date number)** ⎞ extract day,
@**MONTH**              ⎬ month
@**YEAR**               ⎠ and year from date number
@**HOUR**    ⎞ extract hour,
@**MINUTE**  ⎬ minute
@**SECOND**  ⎠ and second from time number
@**TODAY** assigns the date from the DOS date entry.

## Financial functions

These calculate such things as loans, annuities, cash flows and depreciation rates over a period of time. They include:
@**CTERM(int,fv,pv)** the number of compounding periods needed for an investment of *present value* (pv) to grow to *future value* (fv) earning a fixed *periodic interest* rate int.
@**FV** for *future value* and @**PV** for *present value* of an annuity
@**NPV(int,range)** the *present value* of the series of future cash flows in a *range*, discounted at the *periodic interest rate* (int).
@**IRR(guess,range)** the *internal rate of return* for the series of cash flows in the *range*, based on the approximate percentage guess of the IRR.
@**PMT(prin,int,term)** the amount of the periodic payment needed to pay off *principal* (prin) at *periodic interest rate* (int) over the number of payment periods in *term*.

**@RATE(fv,pv,term)** the periodic interest rate necessary for *present value* (pv) to grow to *future value* (fv) over the number of compunding periods in the *term*.

**@SLN(cost,salvage,life)** the *straight-line depreciation* allowance of an asset for one period given the cost, the predicted *salvage value* and *life* of the asset.

**Combining functions**

e.g. **@SUM(C1..C99)-@SUM(D1-D99)** will subtract the sum of columnD from the sum of column C

e.g. **@ROUND(@AVG(J3..J7),0)** will round off the average of cells J3 to J7 with 0 decimal places

Database statistical, string and mathematical functions are not covered in this section.

# Appendix II

## Answer to Activity 26

**Entering the model**

Type in all the labels as suggested. Use the repeat key for the line separators.

Select **/WCS17** to widen column A for the long labels.

Select **/RLR B4 . . G4** to right-justify the monthly headings.

The rest involves formulae work and copying, all of which you have met before!

Select **/WGFF2** to format all the cells to two decimal places.

In B6 type **6500**

Type the unit sales figures into cells B10 . . G10 (*see* note on page 63).

Select **/RFF0 B10 . . G10** for whole numbers.

In B11 type 180 and copy into C11 . . G11.

In E13 type **+B10*B11** (i.e. July's income received three months later (*see* note 2 on page 63)

Copy the formula into F13.G13

In F14 type **30000** (the legacy − *see* note 5 on page 63)

In B16 type @**SUM(B13 . . B15)** to add Sales and other income.

Copy across into C16 . . G16.

In B20 type **60**

Copy to C20 . . G20

Select **/RFF0 B20.G20** for whole numbers

In B22 type **50**

In B23 type **40**

In B24 type **30**

Copy B22 . . B24 to C22 . . G24.

In B26 type @**SUM(B23 . . B24)*B20** (materials excluded − *see* note 7 on page 63).

Copy into C26

In D26 type @**SUM(D22 . . D24)*D20**

Copy into E26 . . G26.

In C28 type **1000** and copy into D28 . . G28

In D29 type **20000** (*see* note 4 on page 63).

Now return to the overdraft in row 30 at the end.

In B32 type @**SUM(B26 . . B31)** to add all the outgoings.

Copy the formula into C32 . . G32.

In B34 type **+B6+B16-B32** (i.e. cash at start plus cash received minus cash paid out).

Copy into C35 . . G35.

In C6 type **+B34** This simply copies the carried forward cash balance from the end of the previous month to start the new one.

Copy into D6 . . G6.

Select **/WCS10** to widen columns D, E and F so that the figures are in view.

In B30 type @**IF(B6<0,@ABS(B6*0.015),0)**

Copy this into C30 . . G30.

This formula means: IF the balance at the start of the month (B6 for July) is <0

THEN multiply that balance by 1.5% ignoring the minus sign (the @ABSolute function).

ELSE 0 − i.e. no overdraft charge as you are in credit

Note that without @ABS you would be paying out less. Think about it! Your bank manager would not be happy!

The results and the full contents list are shown on the following pages so that you can check your work.

```
THE HOTSTUFF HEATING COMPANY
cash-flow analysis July-December 19-8
==================================================================
                    JUL      AUG      SEP       OCT       NOV       DEC

Cash in bank     6500.00  2300.00  -2900.00  -31143.50 -34410.65 -5926.81
------------------------------------------------------------------
CASH INFLOW:

Sales volume         30       40       50        60        80       100
Unit Price       180.00   180.00   180.00    180.00    180.00    180.00

Sales Income                                 5400.00   7200.00   9000.00
Legacy                                                30000.00

Sub-total in        0.00     0.00     0.00    5400.00  37200.00   9000.00
------------------------------------------------------------------
CASH OUTFLOW:

Prodn. Volume        60       60       60        60        60        60
Unit costs:
   materials      50.00    50.00    50.00     50.00     50.00     50.00
   labour         40.00    40.00    40.00     40.00     40.00     40.00
   variables      30.00    30.00    30.00     30.00     30.00     30.00

Total Prodn costs 4200.00 4200.00  7200.00   7200.00   7200.00   7200.00

Fixed O'heads             1000.00  1000.00   1000.00   1000.00   1000.00
New machinery                     20000.00
Overdraft charges   0.00     0.00    43.50    467.15    516.16     88.90

Sub-total out     4200.00  5200.00 28243.50   8667.15   8716.16   8288.90
------------------------------------------------------------------
C/F to Bank       2300.00 -2900.00 -31143.50 -34410.65 -5926.81 -5215.71
==================================================================
```

```
A1: [W17] 'THE HOTSTUFF HEATING COMPANY
A2: [W17] 'cash-flow analysis July-December 19-8
A3: [W17] \=
B3: \=
C3: \=
D3: [W10] \=
E3: [W10] \=
F3: [W10] \=
G3: \=
B4: "JUL
C4: "AUG
D4: [W10] "SEP
E4: [W10] "OCT
F4: [W10] "NOV
G4: "DEC
A6: [W17] 'Cash in bank
B6: 6500
C6: +B34
D6: [W10] +C34
E6: [W10] +D34
F6: [W10] +E34
G6: +F34
A7: [W17] \-
```

```
B7:  \-
C7:  \-
D7:  [W10] \-
E7:  [W10] \-
F7:  [W10] \-
G7:  \-
A8:  [W17] 'CASH INFLOW:
A10: [W17] 'Sales volume
B10: (F0) 30
C10: (F0) 40
D10: (F0) [W10] 50
E10: (F0) [W10] 60
F10: (F0) [W10] 80
G10: (F0) 100
A11: [W17] 'Unit Price
B11: 180
C11: 180
D11: [W10] 180
E11: [W10] 180
F11: [W10] 180
G11: 180
A13: [W17] 'Sales Income
E13: [W10] +B10*B11
F13: [W10] +C10*C11
G13: +D10*D11
A14: [W17] 'Legacy
F14: [W10] 30000
A16: [W17] 'Sub-total in
B16: @SUM(B13..B14)
C16: @SUM(C13..C14)
D16: [W10] @SUM(D13..D14)
E16: [W10] @SUM(E13..E14)
F16: [W10] @SUM(F13..F14)

G16: @SUM(G13..G14)
A17: [W17] \-
B17: \-
C17: \-
D17: [W10] \-
E17: [W10] \-
F17: [W10] \-
G17: \-
A18: [W17] 'CASH OUTFLOW:
A20: [W17] 'Prodn. Volume
B20: (F0) 60
C20: (F0) 60
D20: (F0) [W10] 60
E20: (F0) [W10] 60
F20: (F0) [W10] 60
G20: (F0) 60
A21: [W17] 'Unit costs:
A22: [W17] '  materials
B22: 50
```

```
C22: 50
D22: [W10] 50
E22: [W10] 50
F22: [W10] 50
G22: 50
A23: [W17] '  labour
B23: 40
C23: 40
D23: [W10] 40
E23: [W10] 40
F23: [W10] 40
G23: 40
A24: [W17] '  variables
B24: 30
C24: 30
D24: [W10] 30
E24: [W10] 30
F24: [W10] 30
G24: 30
A26: [W17] 'Total Prodn costs
B26: @SUM(B23..B24)*B20
C26: @SUM(C23..C24)*C20
D26: [W10] @SUM(D22..D24)*D20
E26: [W10] @SUM(E22..E24)*E20
F26: [W10] @SUM(F22..F24)*F20
G26: @SUM(G22..G24)*G20
A28: [W17] 'Fixed O'heads
C28: 1000
D28: [W10] 1000
E28: [W10] 1000
F28: [W10] 1000
G28: 1000
A29: [W17] 'New machinery
D29: [W10] 20000
A30: [W17] 'Overdraft charges
B30: @IF(B6<0,@ABS(B6*0.015),0)
C30: @IF(C6<0,@ABS(C6*0.015),0)

D30: [W10] @IF(D6<0,@ABS(D6*0.015),0)
E30: [W10] @IF(E6<0,@ABS(E6*0.015),0)
F30: [W10] @IF(F6<0,@ABS(F6*0.015),0)
G30: @IF(G6<0,@ABS(G6*0.015),0)
A32: [W17] 'Sub-total out
B32: @SUM(B26..B31)
C32: @SUM(C26..C31)
D32: [W10] @SUM(D26..D31)
E32: [W10] @SUM(E26..E31)
F32: [W10] @SUM(F26..F31)
G32: @SUM(G26..G31)
A33: [W17] \-
B33: \-
C33: \-
D33: [W10] \-
```

```
E33: [W10] \-
F33: [W10] \-
G33: \-
A34: [W17] 'C/F to Bank
B34: +B6+B16-B32
C34: +C6+C16-C32
D34: [W10] +D6+D16-D32
E34: [W10] +E6+E16-E32
F34: [W10] +F6+F16-F32
G34: +G6+G16-G32
A35: [W17] \=
B35: \=
C35: \=
D35: [W10] \=
E35: [W10] \=
F35: [W10] \=
G35: \=
```